Sisters in Spirit

W9-DDV-814

cultural studies
native american   4-

Sisters in Spirit

Haudenosaunee (Iroquois) Influence on Early American Feminists

Sally Roesch Wagner

Introduction by Jeanne Shenandoah

☞

Native Voices

Summertown, Tennessee

Native Voices

Book Publishing Company
P.O. Box 99
Summertown, TN 38483
1-888-260-8458

Copyright 2001 by Sally Roesch Wagner

Cover painting by David Kanietakeron Fadden
Cover design by Warren Jefferson
Book design by Jerry Lee Hutchens

20 19 18 17   6 7 8 9

ISBN 10: 1-57067-121-4   ISBN 13: 978-1-57067-121-0

All rights reserved. No part of this book may be reproduced or uti-
lized in any form by any means, electronic or mechanical, including photocopying or by any information retrieval system without
permission in writing from the publisher. Inquiries should be
addressed to The Book Publishing Company.

Wagner, Sally Roesch.
  Sisters in spirit : Haudenosaunee (Iroquois) influence on early American
      feminists
/ Sally Roesch Wagner.
      p. cm.
Includes bibliographical references and index.
  ISBN 1-57067-121-4
  1. Feminism--United States--History. 2. Feminism--Indian influences.
  3. Women's rights--United States--History. 4. Iroquois philosophy. I.
Title.
  HQ1410 .W35 2001
  305.42'0973--dc21
                            2001003988

We chose to print this title on responsibly harvested paper stock certified by The Forest
Stewardship Council, an independent auditor of responsible forestry practices. For
more information, visit http//us.fsc.org.

To my grandson, Tanner.
May your eyes always be clear
and your ears open.

Photo by Linda Roesch

Acknowledgments

This book is in your hand because of John Kahionhes Fadden. I was so convinced that anything a white woman wrote about Natives would get it wrong that I resolved not to publish anything in this area of research until I was asked to do so—by Native people. I met John at a conference in 1988. He walked out immediately after my paper, and I put my notes in my bag with sinking heart. He'd said everything I needed to know with his back. Others came up to visit and I was about to leave the hall when the door opened and back in came John. He smiled as he walked up to me. "You made me very happy with what you said." My life changed with those words.

John asked for a few business cards to share with folks. When I returned home to California, there was an encouraging letter from his father, Ray, waiting for me. Calls came from other scholars (quickly friends) Bruce Johansen and Don Grinde, and soon, a note from Doug George requesting an article for *Akwesasne Notes*. I sent my conference paper—the first thing I published. Another conference at Cornell and Jose Barreiro asked for an article in *Northeast Indian Quarterly*. With two Native publications requesting work on this topic, I felt that perhaps I wasn't getting it too wrong, and agreed to write an article for a feminist journal, *On the Issues*, working with friend John Stoltenberg, a brilliant editor. These three articles appear in rewritten form in this book.

Two other projects inform the book, both done during "Celebrate '98," that summer when eyes were fastened on Seneca Falls, New York, and the commemoration of the first woman's rights convention held there 150 years before. There was a long-overdue thanks needed, it seemed to me, to the Haudenosaunee women for modeling the position women should occupy. Mary Ellen Snyder, Chief of Interpretation at the Women's Rights National Historical Park, agreed, and arranged for me to write a curriculum for the Park: "Celebrating your Cultural Heritage by Telling the Untold Stories." Mary Kelly Black thoughtfully edited it, while Vivien Rose, Pat Rittenhouse and Joanne Hanley supported it in various ways. Freida Jacques and Stephanie Waterman, from the Onondaga Nation, reviewed it, as did Art Einhorn and Vista Fundamental School in Simi Valley, California, Barbara Marino, Principal.

The title, "Sisters in Spirit," came from an exhibit a group of us produced that summer: Edgar Brown and Robyn Hansen, Julie Uticone, Cheryl Frank and Linda Rosekrans. Bob Venables carefully shaped the words Robyn and I wrote, they will recognize some of them between these covers. The Elizabeth Cady Stanton Foundation sponsored the project, as did The Friends of Ganondagan, Wells College and Eastern National.

The late Alice Papineau generously and gently opened my eyes, as Audrey Shenandoah continues to do. Freida Jacques and her family feed my thoughts as we share meals (and do we ever eat well!)

This book owes everything to Gloria Marvin, who polished my words without ever changing the meaning. Denise Waterman suggested critical changes and held me to my voice, pointing out where I lost it, as only one who lives in an oral tradition would recognize. Laurie Carter Noble encouraged and Paul Waterman kept me laughing. Jerry Hutchens respected every hesitation and every attempt to avoid cultural intrusion, understanding and patiently midwifing the book, creating it in beauty as he wove the visual stories of John Kahionhes Fadden through my words. Jeanne Shenandoah sets the context, so that you may know the purpose of the book, and gifts me with her friendship as we lecture and work together. The words of Tehanetorens (Ray Fadden) begin and end the book, which brings me great honor. And finally, the crowning glory, David Kanietakeron Fadden, provided the cover art. Which seems just right. Three generations of a Mohawk family carry the book: Ray and his son, John, and his son, David. Adopted into the Wolf Clan of the Mohawk nation, Matilda Joslyn Gage would be pleased, I'm sure, as am I. This is the book Julie Uticone dreamed.

Friends all, thank you.

Sally Roesch Wagner

Contents

Introduction

For those of you who are reading this, we hope that the messages inside will help to open your eyes and ears to things that you may have never realized or even thought about, since this type of information has been withheld in the education of all the people. Hopefully it will help you to overcome stereotypes and misunderstandings and gain an appreciation of some of the teachings and behaviors of the Native people that allowed relationships to form between our peoples. These bonds created friendships and movements that made a difference in the future of many women's lives.

We Haudenosaunee live within the traditional structure that we've always had, the structure of equality among all members of our community. Women, men, and children have equal spiritual, human, and political rights. We have equal opportunity to voice opinions or objections to any situation within our community, and we know that our voice will be heard.

And so, when we met these white women so long ago, I am sure that our women were probably shocked at the lack of human equality that these other women had to live under. And we, seeing them as equal—all women as equal—couldn't understand how not only women, but women and children, were living under this totally oppressive situation. How people who had fled their homelands, for exactly the same reason, could appear here on our Turtle Island, our Mother Earth, and bring with them the exact same oppressive behaviors that they had experienced. For the men to walk, set foot on this land and say, "This is mine, I want this, I'm taking this," is an example of how they were thinking.

Read this book and learn from it. It helps you to realize what women have gone through to make a stand for their rightful, equal place on earth. These women raised the children, gave them teachings and influenced them to be caring, respectful people—and still had energy to claim their place on earth, standing equal in all areas of life.

Jeanne Shenandoah,
Onondaga Nation

Who Gets to be Part of History?

"Fourteen Strings of Purple Wampum to Writers about Indians" by Tehanetorens (Ray Fadden)

We hold in our hand fourteen strings of purple wampum. These we hand, one by one, to you—authors of many American history books; writers of cheap, inaccurate, unauthentic, sensational novels; and other writers of fiction who have poisoned the minds of young Americans concerning our people, the Red Race of America; to the producers of many western cowboy and Indian television programs and moving pictures shows; to those Treaty-breakers who delight in dispossessing Indian Peoples by constructing dams on Indian lands in violation of sacred treaties; and to those of this, our country, who are prone to build up the glory of their ancestors on the bonds and life-blood of our Old People:

—With this first string of wampum, we take away the fog that surrounds your eyes and obstructs your view, that you may see the truth concerning our people!

—With this second string of wampum, we pull away from your imprisoned minds the cobwebs, the net that prevents you from dealing justice to our people!

—With this third piece of wampum, we cleanse your hearts of revenge, selfishness, and injustice, that you may create love instead of hate!

—With this fourth string of wampum, we wash the blood of our people from your hands, that you may know the clasp of true friendship and sincerity!

—With this fifth string of wampum, we shrink your heads down to that of normal man, we cleanse your minds of the abnormal conceit and love of self that has caused you to walk blindly among the dark people of the world.

—With this sixth string of wampum, we remove your garments of gold, silver, and greed, that you may don the apparel of generosity, hospitality, and humanity!

11

—With this seventh string of wampum, we remove the dirt that fills your ears so you may hear the story and truth of our people!

—With this eighth string of wampum, we straighten your tongues of crookedness, that in the future you may speak the truth concerning Indian People!

—With this ninth string of wampum, we take away the dark clouds from the face of the sun, that its rays may purify your thoughts, that you may look forward and see America, instead of backward toward Europe!

—With this tenth string of wampum, we brush away the rough stones and sticks from your path, that you may walk erect as the first American whose name you have defamed and whose country you now occupy!

—With this eleventh string of wampum, we take away from your hands your implements of destruction—guns, bombs, firewater, diseases—and place in them instead the Pipe of Friendship and Peace, that you may sow brotherly love rather than bitter hate and injustice!

—With this twelfth string of wampum, we build you a new house with many windows and no mirrors, that you may look out and see the life and purpose of your nearest neighbor, the American Indian!

—With this thirteenth string of wampum, we tear down the wall of steel and stone you have built around the TREE OF PEACE, that you may take shelter beneath its branches!

—With this fourteenth string of wampum, we take from the hencoop the eagle that you have imprisoned, that this noble bird may once again fly in the sky over America!

I, *Te-ha-ne-to-rens*, say this![1]

Wampum—purple and white shell beads strung or sewn onto belts of material—carries the history of the people. (European settlers corrupted wampum into currency.) Wampum also instructs in the importance of responsibilities. Mohawk historian Te-ha-ne-to-rens (Ray Fadden) guides non-Native writers in what we need to do to prepare ourselves to write. His words are fueled by indignation at the damage white writers have caused Indians.

I read Ray's words when I sit down to write about Native people. They remind me that the greatest likelihood is that, as a white person, I will get it wrong; the highest probability is that I will cause damage. Filled with centuries of justifications for genocide, popular as well as academic stereotypes that mask the truth, and a cultural belief that I have the right to tell someone else's story my way, I am dangerous. If I wish to create accurate, inclusive history I must first open my ears to hear, my eyes to see, and my mind to absorb the story before me.[2]

I am not alone. We EuroAmericans are filled with the poison of misinformation. Great gaps of knowledge accompany the lies. Omissions teach us equally, and more insidiously, than misinformation. The lesson of exclusion is clear. Groups of people *included* in the interpretation of history are respected, while *excluded* groups are outsiders and can easily be ignored. If our teachers do not tell us about a group of people, we assume they are unimportant.

The message of omissions is an educational foundation of racism. Through the silence in our education, many of us have learned *not* to listen to the histories of people of color, women, and other excluded groups. We have been trained to pay attention to what is "important" and to ignore what is not. Therefore it is not enough to be exposed to new information. We must first be able to receive it. Essentially, we must remake ourselves in order to absorb what we have been taught from childhood to ignore.

It is important, of course, to know that "In 1492, Columbus sailed the Ocean Blue," as that date marked the beginning of EuroAmerican settlement in this hemisphere. However, recognition of diversity comes about when we revisit the Columbus story, identify the participants, and consider how they each experienced the event. If indigenous people do not exist in the story we are told, we conclude their story has no importance and neither do they. We need to ask basic and simple questions to break this silence. What was the view from the shore? What did those who were living on Turtle Island (the Native Americans' term for North America) see as the boats approached and the occupants disembarked? How did each group interpret what they saw? What was going on that both the Natives and those on the boats did not have "eyes" to see? Columbus described the world he "discovered" as a virtual utopia — the happy, well-fed, peaceful inhabitants a mirror contrast to the militaristic, cruel, harsh world from which he had sailed. What would have happened if he had asked, "How do you do this?" rather than scheming how best to exploit the Natives and their resources?

Multidimensional Thinking

Human interactions are complex, and there is never one way to tell a story. In fact, people throughout history have experienced conflicts and friendships simultaneously. It should come as no surprise then, that in our history, we find intermarriage among cultural groups at war with each other. Similarly, EuroAmerican women taken captive by Native American nations often chose to continue to live as adopted members of the nation rather than return to the EuroAmerican world. Their enemies had become family; their identity Indian.

Influence is a basic theme of history. As groups come into contact (in violence and/or friendship) they influence each other and adapt to one another. Each group takes on the others' ways. Influence does not necessarily mean bias-free interaction. We can believe we are superior to a group of people at the same time we are influenced by them. Rap music's popularity with white youth does not mean we have eliminated racism, any more than the popularity of jazz did with their parents.

The Historical Development of History

There is nothing inherent or inevitable about history. Created by people, it is shaped by the same socio-political-economic forces that determine the telling of it. History changes, like institutions, when people demand change. As excluded groups seek inclusion in institutions, they also celebrate their histories, demanding to be remembered. United States history has gone through phases in the last fifty years reflecting cultural and social shifts toward greater inclusion and diversity.

14

The history of powerlessness: Great white men, great victories.

Baby boomers grew up learning a history of the winners, from the winners' perspective. A history told for the benefit of those in the position to decide how history should be told. This phase of history gave the message that wars are the most important events. Dates had importance in and of themselves, without context. Indirectly, this phase of history also conveyed the message that the only people that matter are wealthy white men and that common people have no influence over the course of events.

Stories of the silenced: Victim history.

As various groups began to demand their civil rights during the 1960s, they also demanded to tell their version of history. From people of color, from women, children, gays and lesbians, from differently-abled and poor people, unfolded a story of injustice, violation, and victimization. Viewing the underbelly of the "great white men" story revealed the price paid by those who were subjugated. After initial resistance to these stories, it became possible to comprehend the extent of the exclusion and destruction and depth of oppression each group suffered.

Stories of empowerment: Survival, resistance, and overcoming.

Oppressed people survived; and more than that, they accomplished seemingly impossible tasks and successfully demanded improvements in their condition. Courage, adaptability, and strength of spirit are revealed by their stories. Despite the overwhelming institutional power of slavery, for example, African Americans maintained integrity, families, and community.

Friendship and influence in the midst of oppression.

Recognition of historical injustices opened the way to see the triumphs of those who resisted, overcame nearly overwhelming odds, and survived. Most recently, we have begun to explore the unexpected and largely unknown stories of friendships established during colonization and coexistence, and of the way groups influenced each other. The revelation that our Founding Fathers received tutelage in democracy from the Haudenosaunee (Iroquois) is one eye-opening example. Native influence on the non-Native woman's rights movement is another story of friendship and influence.

Identifying the Players and the Issues

Who first comes to mind when we mention suffrage? *Susan B. Anthony.* Her name is linked with the vote; the two have become synonymous. If we look at the story of the victory won (woman's struggle for the vote), Susan B. Anthony's name is primary, but this story is not a complete history. If we look beyond the vote we find a much broader movement for the rights, privileges, and protections under the government in which suffrage was the capstone. Suffrage, in turn, was only one of many issues raised by the nineteenth century woman's movement ranging from an acknowledgment of the Motherhood (as well as the Fatherhood) of God to a drive for a woman's right to control her own body. From a campaign for equal pay for equal work to a demand for an end to marital rape and battering, activists a hundred years ago articulated most of the demands of the current feminist movement. Yet we know little of this bigger story. We may be uncomfortable telling this fuller history because we have not yet resolved these questions, and people on each side still feel passionately about them today.

We may not find anyone today who believes that woman's struggle for the vote was a radical and heretical challenge to the God-ordained authority of man. However, a majority of the population, male and female, believed this to be true at the time of the 1848 Seneca Falls Convention. We proudly tell the tale of women in the early 1900s chaining themselves to the White House fence for the vote. Yet we may not celebrate the courage of the friends and colleagues of Susan B. Anthony who served time in jail for telling women how they could prevent conception. It is easy to tell the story of Susan B. Anthony and the successful struggle for the vote. When we move beyond these "finished" stories, however, telling the historical truth may take courage and care, because unresolved issues create controversy. We run the risk of being fired or not having our textbook accepted if we tell the history of radical challenge to the status quo. Such examination, however, is at the heart of decision-making in a democracy. When we knowingly avoid teaching the history of controversial issues, we deprive citizens of the tools needed to make wise decisions.

We may teach about slavery in a way that makes it a safe, distant story for white people. Granted, it was a terrible part of our history (we may justify), but it's behind us now, and the white people who supported slavery were totally unlike us today. An hour of unease in a classroom or museum and we can move on, reassuring ourselves that—had we lived then—our home would have been a station on the Underground Railroad. In reality, it probably would *not* have been. Most of us would have been silent on slavery. Many of us would have actively favored it. Only a few would have had the courage to stand up to charges of being a "Godless, man-stealing, law-breaking thief" hurled against us if we were early abolitionists. At a time when the Constitution had slavery built into it and ministers preached that slaves should obey their masters, those who opposed slavery had to resist the law and, generally speaking, the church as well. Abolitionists were accused of stealing the property of slave owners when they helped fugitive slaves to escape. Anti-slavery activists were considered radicals who upset the social, political, and religious order of society.

That information may cause us to question the institutions that sustained slavery. Is it possible that the churches upholding slavery in the 1830s might be equally unclear about similar issues of justice today? Ethical people opposed slavery by breaking the laws that sustained it. Do we have a similar moral responsibility to break contemporary laws we consider unjust?

The "comfortable" history of slavery ends with the 13th Amendment, which declared slavery illegal in the United States. The legacy of personal and institutional racism left behind by slavery is the uncomfortable story. Similarly, the "safe" version of the woman's rights story is the victory of the 19th Amendment and the constitutional protection of women's voting rights. This is the story of Susan B. Anthony and her life's work. For a fuller story of the struggle for women's rights, we must look to other, lesser-known figures who have been written out of history.

Elizabeth Cady Stanton presents us with a starting place. Equal in importance and reputation to Anthony during her lifetime, Stanton was nearly lost to history until the work of the Elizabeth Cady Stanton Foundation and the Women's Rights National Historical Park in Seneca Falls restored her to memory over these past two decades.

Following the leadership of the Stanton Foundation, the Matilda Joslyn Gage Foundation carries the mission of returning Gage to her rightful place in history as well. Gage was the third member of the suffrage "triumvirate" along with Stanton and Anthony. The three women shared leadership positions in the National Woman Suffrage Association and edited the first three volumes of the *History of Woman Suffrage.* While Anthony concentrated on achieving the vote, Gage and Stanton lived a different story—one in which, as Gage said, "the laws, civil and social, each equally burdensome, are of church origin, and not until the church is destroyed will women be freed."[3] Stanton shared Gage's strong feelings about organized religion, charging that: "Every form of religion that has breathed upon the earth has degraded women."[4]

Gage went further, maintaining: "In the name of religion, the worst crimes against humanity have ever been perpetrated."[5] Writing to a friend, Stanton confided, "as I have passed from the political to the religious phrase of this question, I now see more clearly than ever, that the arch enemy to woman's freedom skulks behind the altar . . . to rouse woman to a sense of her degradation under the Canon law and church discipline, is the work that interests me most, and to which I prepare to devote the sunset of my life."[6] Gage devoted her later years to the same work, and concluded: "All thoughtful persons . . . must be aware of the historical fact that the prevailing religious idea in regard to woman has been the basis of all their restrictions and degradation. It underlies political, legal, educational, industrial, and social disabilities of whatever character and nature."[7]

If we eliminate Gage and Stanton's sharp criticisms of institutional, organized religion, are we telling the full truth of their work in the woman's rights movement? Their institutional analysis of oppression extended beyond religion. "Society is based on this four-fold bondage of woman—Church, State, Capital, and Society—making liberty and equality for her antagonistic to every organized institution," they wrote in the *History of Woman Suffrage.*[8] The two women shared similar ideas about the oppressive nature of each institution.

STATE

> **Stanton:** Would to God you could know the burning indignation that fills woman's soul when she turns over

the pages of your statute books, and sees there how like feudal barons you freemen hold your women.[9] I do not feel like rejoicing over any privileges already granted to my sex, until all our rights are conceded and secured and the principle of equality recognized and proclaimed, for every step that brings us to a more equal plane with man but makes us more keenly feel the loss of those rights we are still denied. . . . May we now safely prophesy justice, liberty, equality for our daughters ere another centennial birthday shall dawn upon us.[10]

Gage: A proper self-respect cannot inhere in any person under governmental control of others. Unless the person so governed constantly maintains a system of rebellion in thought or deed, the soul gradually becomes debased and the finest principles of human nature suffer a rapid process of disintegration.[11]

CAPITAL

Stanton: Married women are upper servants without wages.[12] Under the present competitive system existence is continual war; the law is each for himself, starvation and death for the hindmost. . . . It is impossible to have 'equal rights for all' under our present competitive system. . . . The few have no right to the luxuries of life, while the many are denied its necessities.[13]

Gage: It has been truthfully declared that England protects its hunting dogs kept for their master's pleasure far better than it protects the women and children of its working classes.[14] Man, in thrusting the enforcement of his 'curse' upon woman in Christian lands has made her the great unpaid laborer of the world. In European countries and in the United States, we find her everywhere receiving less pay than man for the same kind and quality of work . . . the church teaching that woman was made for man still exerts its poisonous influence, still destroys woman. . . . Not alone employers and male laborers oppress woman but legislation is frequently invoked to prevent her entering certain occupations.[15]

SOCIETY

> **Stanton**: Society as organized today under the man power is one grand rape of womanhood.[16]

> **Gage**: Although our country makes great professions in regard to general liberty, yet the right to particular liberty, natural equality, and personal independence, of two great portions of this country, is treated, from custom, with the greatest contempt; and color in the one instance, and sex in the other, are brought as reasons why they should be so derided; and the mere mention of such natural rights is frowned upon, as tending to promote sedition and anarchy.[17]

How can we best present significant women of history whose ideas are so profoundly challenging? Unfortunately, we often find it easier to not invite them to the history table. Anthony is a well-behaved guest; we ask her instead. However, we make a political decision when we choose to tell only safe or incomplete history. Democracy requires an enlightened citizenry, people who understand their place in the evolving history of issues about which they must decide. We rob the democratic process when we lie, through omission, about history. How do we present an accurate and complete story of our past? Stanton gives direction: "Reformers who are always compromising have not yet grasped the idea that truth is the only safe ground to stand upon." Truth in history is the complete story. We need to cultivate the courage to tell the full stories, along with encouraging the development of a respectful, open mind to hear them.

What is in a Name?

To fill the voids left by silence and misinformation, we begin with basic questions. For example, where did the name Indian originate? What we find is that *Indian* stands as a singular example of the arrogance of someone who believed he had the right—by virtue of a presumed cultural superiority—to name another group of people. One

"The few have no right to the luxuries of life, while the many are denied its necessities."

Elizabeth Cady Stanton

interpretation is that Christopher Columbus, not altogether a first-rate navigator, apparently thought he was in the Indies and deduced that the people greeting him must be Indians. Another version holds that he acknowledged the near-sacred state of the Native people he encountered with the name *in dios*. Whatever the reasons for the name, Columbus believed he had the right to name the people, as he believed he had the right to claim their land. Did it ever occur to him to ask them what they called themselves? Would he have had ears to hear their answer? Each successive wave of European conquerors and settlers played the naming game. They gave names of their choosing to Native nations (such as Sioux and Iroquois), and Christian names to the indigenous children they forced into their boarding schools in order to "Christianize and civilize" them.

Members of the dominant culture often become irritated with the process of peeling off layers of historical paint hiding the true names of indigenous people. Not recognizing the terrible appropriation of self identity inflicted in a false, other-imposed name, they huff at a "political correctness" that requires them to change their language.

Self-naming is, of course, a critical part of the process of creating a diverse culture. The cultural change in names may happen in stages, as we work our way through levels of disrespect. Small animal and fruit names for women are no longer acceptable. We have given up saying "girl" in addressing a fifty-year-old woman and "boy" for a fifty-year-old African American man. "Nigger" and later "Negro" have both been dropped. The self-defined term "Black" proudly reclaimed the very physical characteristic that EuroAmericans used as the basis for enslaving people. "African American" emerged later as a more appropriate term for establishing a nation of diversity.

Native American served to replace the conquering name, Indian, by clarifying who was here first. Some now prefer to use Native, indigenous, or First Nation. Others suggest another term, American Indian, to firmly hold the government to nation-to-nation treaties made with American Indian nations.

While a rigid language suggests a static culture, the changes in our language herald a power shift, mirroring and furthering the social revolution we are undergoing. Unfortunately, we have few linguistic etiquette books, so we stumble along the best we can. One rule: when in doubt about what to call a person or group, don't tie up their time and energy in asking. Read what they have to say. Then sift carefully and slowly through the multiple answers, knowing that this is not a trivial matter. Laughter always helps the tension, and American Indian humor is legendary: "We're just glad Columbus didn't think he was in Turkey!" they joke.

The issue of linguistic oppression is not new to our time. Matilda Joslyn Gage, arguably the most important scholar of the suffrage movement, wrote in 1893: "When America first became known to white men as the New World, within the limits of what is now called New York state existed one of the oldest known republics in the world, a confederacy of Five Nations when first formed, which added tribes to its numbers as its successor, the American republic, adds states to its Union."[18] Gage realized that whether one described this as the Old or New World depended on perspective, and acknowledged that it "became known to white men" as the New. Significantly, Gage's presentation of American history did not begin with the presence of white men.

Clear as she was about the Old World perspective, Gage did not understand the distinction between tribes and nations. Harriet Maxwell Converse, a friend of Gage, did. Converse explained that the difference between tribes and nations was one "not generally understood, the two terms being frequently confounded." The significance rested in nation sovereignty. Converse explained: "The Seneca Nation is . . . as distinct among Indians as France, Germany, and England are distinct among the nations of Europe."[19] Language, she understood, has critical political consequences. Treaties were made with sovereign American Indian nations, not with tribes. However, if no "nations" are recognized, there are no treaties, and the use of the word *tribe* instead of *nation* has the political effect of erasing treaty obligations.

What Do We Call the People Who Influenced the Suffragists?

Having identified the need to find the missing players, we ask, who it is that may have influenced the suffragists? Once we identify them, we run into the question of name. The quick reply, "the Iroquois," uses an imposed name, not the name the people call themselves, which is the "Haudenosaunee, the People of the Longhouse."

"The Six Nations," Converse told her readers, comprised "one of the most powerful confederacies ever known." It "included the Onondagas, the Cayugas, the Senecas, the Mohawks, and the Oneidas. The Tuscaroras were added in 1723. The name Iroquois was not their proper Indian name but was derived, I believe, from the French and has been used instead of Ho-de-man-san-ne."[20] [Her spelling] Converse's description clarified not only the proper name but the confusion that resulted from the Five Nations Confederacy adding a sixth nation after its founding, when the Tuscaroras, after nearly being destroyed by colonists, took safety under the tree of peace and joined the Confederacy.

New York Governor DeWitt Clinton spelled the name, Ho-de-no-sau-nee, which meant "the People of the Longhouse, from the circumstance that they likened their political structure to a long tenement or dwelling."[21]

Gage recognized another name the Haudenosaunee use for indigenous people: "To themselves the Five Nations were known as the Ongwe Honwe, that is, a people surpassing all others."[22]

"The Iroquois call themselves the *real people*," Minnie Myrtle wrote, "and in speeches or conversation, if allusion is made to white people, they say invariably 'our younger brethren.'"[23]

It is instructive to find that these self-chosen, inclusive names, well known to non-Natives a hundred years ago, have somehow become lost in the dusty archives and seldom appear in books today.

Haudenosaunee is the name (and accepted spelling today) for the Six Nations of the Confederacy, but it is not recognizable to most non-Native people, so completely has the power to name been usurped. Should we use the self-chosen name, knowing few will understand or should we use the imposed name that has nearly universal recognition? A third option presents itself: use both. We could begin with the commonly recognized name, Iroquois, and follow it with the chosen name in parentheses, like this: *The Iroquois (Haudenosaunee) Influence on the Early Woman's Rights Movement*. However, parentheses are an aside, a brief interruption in the flow of the narrative. Notice the difference when we present the names the other way around: *The Haudenosaunee (Iroquois) Influence on the Early Woman's Rights Movement*. Haudenosaunee now stands as the proper term; the word Iroquois is included to assist those who do not recognize it.

Language Evolves to Reflect the Way People Change

Savage—a EuroAmerican word implying a lower degree of civilization—was widely used in the 19th Century to describe Native people.

The name the people call themselves, which is the "Haudenosaunee, the People of the Longhouse."

How did this word pass out of use? We look to the suffragists and their acquaintances for a part of the answer.

Minnie Myrtle lived with Laura and Ashur Wright, missionaries to the Seneca nation whose writings were quoted by Stanton. Myrtle questioned the use of the term "savage" in her popular 1855 book, *The Iroquois; or, The Bright Side of Indian Character:*

> A people like the Iroquois who had a government, estab-
> lished offices, a system of religion eminently pure and

spiritual, a code of honor and laws of hospitality excelling those of all other nations, should be considered something better than savage, or utterly barbarous.

Myrtle quoted an eminent Spanish legal authority, Zurita, who spent nineteen years among the Aztecs, and was as indignant that they should be called barbarian as she was when the Haudenosaunee were similarly labeled:

> It is an epithet which could come from no one who had personal knowledge of the capacity of the people or their institutions, and which in some respects is quite as well merited by Europeans. If the Aztecs did not deserve the term barbarians, surely I shall be thought just in denying the term savage to belong to the Iroquois; and from their mythology, if nothing else, it is evident that they were destitute neither of genius nor of poetry.[24]

Eventually such challenges to the white supremacy embedded in the word *savage* caused the term to drop from common usage. The presence of equally offensive words in our present language reveals how far we have yet to go in our evolution toward equality.

Squaw, an insulting slang term which French fur trappers created from an Algonquin word referring to female genitalia, is an example of a word on its way out of the English language. Two teenage Ojibwa girls led a successful crusade to have Minnesota remove the word from all place names in the state. The issue is not new. Native American women have been protesting the use of the offensive term for at least a hundred years, as this 1890 story in the *Onondaga Standard* demonstrates:

> By the way, a little note here will not be found out of place to those readers who expect at some future day to come into contact with Indians, when they shall have to, perhaps surrender all the nicety of good usages to appear favorable in the estimation of the Indians, only to be embarrassed by the horrible outbreak of calling an Indian woman 'Squaw,' and find when too late two piercing jet black eyes resting upon some troubled countenance, as

much as to say, "What is a squaw? Why do you call me a squaw? You are a squaw yourself! It is a vulgar expression; don't use it; the Indians don't use it; why should others?"[25]

The Oregon Geographic Names Board is changing the name of a prominent peak from Squaw Butte to Paiute Butte. A South Dakota official faced sanctions from the Governor for telling a joke using the insulting term. Within our children's lifetime, we will probably see this offensive word eliminated from public use. Unfortunately, many suffragists must not have been aware of its meaning, for they used the word. It will appear in this book as they wrote it with a [sic] beside it to remind us of its inappropriateness.

Haudenosaunee Women: An Inspiration to Early Feminists

The woman's rights movement was born in the territory of the Haudenosaunee in 1848. Were the suffrage leaders influenced by Native women? Was there a connection between the authority and responsibilities held by Haudenosaunee women and the vision of the woman's rights movement?

Elizabeth Cady Stanton, Matilda Joslyn Gage, and Lucretia Mott were among the leaders of the woman's rights cause. Stanton and Mott organized the 1848 Seneca Falls Convention. Gage joined the movement in 1852 along with Susan B. Anthony. During her lifetime, Gage was recognized as the third member of the suffrage leadership "triumvirate" with Anthony and Stanton, but today she is less well known. Recognizing Gage's formative role in developing feminist theory opens a new story of women's rights.

Gage wrote extensively about the Haudenosaunee, especially the position of women in what she termed their "matriarchate" or system of "mother-rule." She was working on a book about the Haudenosaunee when she died in 1898. In 1875, while president of the National Woman Suffrage Association, Gage wrote a series of newspaper articles on the Haudenosaunee. The editor of the *New York Evening Post* said that Gage expressed "an exhibition of ardent devotion to the cause of women's rights which is very proper in the president of the . . . Suffrage Association and gives prominence to the fact that in the old days when the glory of the famous confederation . . . was at its height, the power and importance of women were recognized by the allied tribes."[1]

Spanning a 20-year period, Gage introduced readers to the Six Nations of the Iroquois Confederacy in articles, the newspaper she edited (*The National Citizen and Ballot Box*, 1878-1881) and her magnum opus (*Woman, Church and State*, 1893). She explained the form of government of the Mohawk, Oneida, Onondaga, Cayuga, Seneca, and Tuscarora and their confederacy of peace.

> The famous Iroquois Indians, or Six Nations, which at the discovery of America held sway from the Great Lakes to the Tombigbe river, from the Hudson to the Ohio . . . showed alike in form of government, and in social life, reminiscences of the Matriarchate.[2]

The clarity of understanding of Indian nation sovereignty that Gage displayed in an editorial in her newspaper in 1878 is a source of wonder to Native people today:

> Our Indians are in reality foreign powers, though living among us. With them our country not only has treaty obligations, but pays them, or professes to, annual sums in consideration of such treaties. . . . Compelling them to become citizens would be like the forcible annexation of Cuba, Mexico, or Canada to our government, and as unjust.[3]

Haudenosaunee and EuroAmerican Women in 1848

Matilda Joslyn Gage and Elizabeth Cady Stanton, the major theoreticians of the woman's rights movement, claimed that the society in which they lived was based on the oppression of women.

Haudenosaunee society, on the other hand, was organized to maintain a balance of equality between women and men. Shown here are the contrasting differences between the two worlds of women who lived side-by-side in this region of upstate New York in 1848.

Haudenosaunee:

SOCIAL

Children are members of the mother's clan

Violence against women not part of culture, and dealt with seriously when occurs

Clothing fosters health, freedom of movement and independence

Woman's responsibilities have a spiritual basis

ECONOMIC

Work satisfying, done communally

Responsible for agriculture as well as home life

Work done under the direction of the women, working together

Each woman controls her own personal property

SPIRITUAL

"Sky Woman" the spiritual being, catalyst for the world we see

Mother Earth and women spiritually interrelated

Women have responsibilities in ceremony
Responsibilities in balance with those of men

EuroAmerican:

SOCIAL

Children are the sole property of fathers

Husbands have legal right and religious responsibility to physically discipline wives

Clothing is restrictive, unhealthy and dangerous

Woman's subordination has a religious foundation

ECONOMIC

Work drudgery, isolated

Responsible for home, but subordinate to husband

Work done under authority of the husband

No rights to her own property, body, or children

SPIRITUAL

No female in the godhead

Spirituality not connected to the earth

Women forbidden to speak in churches
Responsibilities subordinate to men's authority

POLITICAL

Women choose their chief

Women hold key political offices (eg., clan mothers)

Confederacy law ensures woman's political authority

Decision making by consensus, everyone has a voice

POLITICAL

Illegal for women to vote

Women excluded from political office

Common law defines married women as "dead in the law"

Decision making by men, majority rules

War chief holding woman's nominating wampum belt.

How Well Did These Culturally Different Women Know Each Other?

Even though they lived in very different cultural, economic, spiritual, and political worlds during the early 1800s, EuroAmerican settlers in Central/Western New York were, at most, one person away from direct familiarity with Iroquois people. The Haudenosaunee continued their ancient practice of adopting individuals of other nations, and many white residents of New York (including Matilda Joslyn Gage) carried adoptive Indian names. Friendships and visiting were commonplace activities between Natives and non-Natives. Newspapers routinely printed news from American Indian country. Each local history book began with a lengthy account of the first inhabitants of the land. These three leaders of the woman's rights movement—Stanton, Gage, and Mott—were among those who had a personal connection with the Haudenosaunee.

Lucretia Mott visited the Seneca Nation in June 1848

Lucretia Mott and her husband James visited the Cattaraugus community in June 1848, just before taking part in the historic Seneca Falls Convention in July.

Matilda Joslyn Gage was adopted into the Wolf Clan of the Mohawk Nation

"I received the name of Ka-ron-ien-ha-wi, or 'Sky Carrier,' or *She who holds the sky*." She wrote. "It is a clan name of the wolves."[4]

Elizabeth Cady Stanton's cousin was named for an Oneida Chief and her closest Seneca Falls neighbor was an adopted Onondagan.

Elizabeth Cady Stanton's cousin, Peter Skenandoah Smith, was named for an Oneida friend of the family, Chief Skenandoah. In addition, her nearest Seneca Falls neighbor, Oren Tyler, came from Onondaga, where he "had friendly dealings" with the people there and was adopted by them. He spoke their language fluently, and parties of Onondagans passing through Seneca Falls to sell their bead work and baskets "sought out their 'brother,' as they called Capt. Tyler, who always befriended them."[5]

Three generations of the Wolf Clan.

Forerunners

Gage, Stanton, and Mott were not alone among reformers to respect Native ways of life, nor were they the first. Many nineteenth-century feminists felt a strong kinship with Native Americans. Frances Wright, for example, was the first woman to publicly speak before audiences of men and women in the United States on woman's rights—twenty years before there was an organized woman's movement. Together with Robert Dale Owen, she edited a reform paper, the *Free Enquirer*, in the late 1820s. Practicing a decidedly pro-Indian editorial policy, their paper carried articles on the Cherokee alphabet, an interview with the Seneca sachem Red Jacket, a comparison of Christian and Indian "superstitions" (Christianity lost badly by contrast), and a strongly-worded protest against a threatened attack on the Winnebago and Potawatomi nations by the United States army. "The whites are more apt to commit first aggressions than the Indians," the editors contended. Owen was deeply committed to woman's rights. He and Lydia Maria Child, another prototype feminist

33

most commonly known for her anti-slavery writing, were particularly moved by the fact that Indian men did not rape.

Women Writers

Many non-Native women studied and wrote about the Haudenosaunee—professional ethnographers such as Alice Fletcher and Erminnie Smith, along with amateur ones—women like Gage—who had developed an interest in, and friendships with Haudenosaunee women. Several dozen of these women often wrote with a depth of understanding which would, no doubt, have been recognized and respected into this century had they been men.

Laura M. Sheldon Wright, wife of a missionary at Cattaraugus, for example, published a *Dictionary of the Seneca Language* around 1835.[7]

Harriet Maxwell Converse, the woman who arranged for Gage to be adopted into the Wolf Clan of the Mohawk nation, wrote extensively for New York papers. While her *Myths and Legends of the New York State Iroquois* (1908) has been criticized for being romanticized, her newspaper articles were straightforward and highly descriptive. They also document her extensive support and lobbying work for the Haudenosaunee. Converse "has ready for the press a volume of lyrics, sonnets, and Indian myth songs," Harriet Phillips Eaton wrote Gage in the 1890s. Eaton, who was Gage's cousin, also wrote about the Iroquois.[8]

Helen F. Troy was adopted by Thomas and Electa Thomas into the Snipe Clan of the Onondaga nation in 1894 and given the name Garwen-ne-sho or "Spirit Dipping into the Silent Waters" in 1905. *The New York Herald* announced that "Mrs. Troy is at present at work on and is soon to have published an elaborate translation of the 'Book of the Sacred Wampum,' or the Iroquois Bible, also a dictionary for use in the colleges, of the Onondaga and Mohawk tongues with their equivalent meanings in English." The book was the result of fifteen years of research.[9]

Erminnie A. Smith was appointed by the Smithsonian Institution to study the Six Nations in 1880. She "lived among the Indians to study their habits and folklore and was so well-liked by the Tuscaroras that she was adopted into the White Bear Clan" and given the name of Ka-tie-tio-sta-knost, meaning "Beautiful Flower." At the time of her death six years later, she was working towards completion of an Iroquois dictionary containing 15,000 classified words—6,000 of the Tuscaroras, 3,000 of the Onondagas, and a thousand each of the Oneidas and Senecas. She was just beginning her work with the Cayuga's language when she died.[10]

Her assistant, J. N. B. Hewitt, a Tuscarora who became a respected expert at the Bureau of Ethnology, completed the dictionary, calling Smith "a superbly gifted scholar."[11] Horatio Hale said Smith "had pursued studies which in Ethnology alone would make any man famous." The first woman elected to the New York Academy of Sciences, Smith was also a member of the Association for the Advancement of Science, the English Anthropological Society, and one of the leaders of the woman's club, Sorosis—of which Gage was also a member. A contributor to various scientific journals,[12] Smith's *Myths of the Iroquois*, originally published in 1883, is in print again today.[13]

Mary Elizabeth Beauchamp was the sister of William M. Beauchamp, who, according to *The Dictionary of American Biography* "became, among white men, the greatest authority on the history and institutions of the Iroquois. In a sense he was the successor of Lewis Morgan in this field." Mary Elizabeth, who also wrote about the Haudenosaunee, was her brother's secretary. In one of her newspaper articles, she wrote:

> I believe I have mentioned the fact that women are treated with great respect among the Onondagas, and in fact are usually supposed to rule. When I came to teaching my little folks to read the catechism, I found that in the Fifth Commandment, they invariably put the *mother* before the *father*, even after repeated reading and corrections.[14]

William Beauchamp mentioned in *Iroquois Folk Lore* that he had procured for the State Library an "interesting series of Seneca tales from Miss Myra E. Trippe of Salamanca, NY. Unfortunately," he continued, "they were destroyed, along with the *Moravian Journals* I sent there at the same time."[15]

While Gage read Morgan, Lafitte, Schoolcraft, Catlin, and Clark on the Iroquois, she *knew* the Beauchamp family. There were strong family ties between the two. Gage wrote for Beauchamp's father's paper, and his daughter-in-law wrote a song, "The Battle Hymn of the Suffragists" in honor of Gage.

Newspapers

A wide range of information on the Haudenosaunee was readily available through newspapers. The local Syracuse paper, the *Onondaga Standard*—which Gage read—reported everything from condolence ceremonies to council proceedings to spiritual ceremonies. When legislation was introduced to break up the land of the Six Nations into individual ownership, protests that came from the Onondaga nation were published in full by the paper, along with the names of all the signatures to the petitions.

The level of sophistication of these newspaper stories indicates that the average reader in upstate New York 100 years ago possessed knowledge about the Iroquois that, among non-Natives, is held by only a relatively small number of scholars today. The newspaper articles assumed, for example, that the readers knew the process by which a chief was raised up and what comprised a condolence ceremony.[16]

When Gage picked up her daily paper, she read how the Haudenosaunee ginseng trade with China was threatened by political events in that country. A dispute when two chiefs were raised up simultaneously brought non-Native readers into the question of which was the legitimate one. When Anton Dvorak came to the United States to write his New World Symphony, he suggested that indigenous music is the true voice of America; a Syracuse University professor gave a lecture supporting that thesis from his study of Iroquois music.

With so many writers and newspaper stories creating such a sophisticated level of general knowledge, it comes as no surprise that when reformers like Matilda Joslyn Gage looked for a model upon which to base their vision of an egalitarian world, they quickly found their well-known Native neighbors. And what did they find? What was revealed to the suffragists about women's relative status in these two contrasting worlds? What did they have eyes to see?

The Untold Story

I did not set out to look for this connection, this link between early suffragists and Native peoples. In truth, if someone had suggested it to me when I taught my first women's studies class in 1969, I would have scoffed at yet one more "romantic Indian" story. I had a single question, basic to feminist history: *How did the radical suffragists come to their vision, a vision not of Band-Aid reform but of a reconstituted world completely transformed?* Surely I should know the answer—after all, I had helped found one of the nation's first women's studies programs (at California State University, Sacramento) and received one of the first doctorates for work in women's studies (from the University of California, Santa Cruz). I was credentialed but I was baffled.

For twenty years I had immersed myself in the writings of early United States women's-rights activists Matilda Joslyn Gage (1826-1898) and Elizabeth Cady Stanton (1815-1902), yet I could not fathom how they dared to dream their revolutionary dream. Living under the ideological hegemony of nineteenth-century United States, these women had no say in government, religion, economics, or social life. Whatever made them think that human harmony, respect for women's lives, and equal rights for women were achievable? Surely these white women, living under conditions they likened to slavery, did not receive their vision in a vacuum.

Certainly there was a European foundation for American feminism. Gage, regarded as "one of the most logical, fearless, and scientific writers of her day," maintained that European women, along with their male supporters, had waged a four-hundred-year struggle for woman's rights.[1] She asserted this past came to the forefront during the American Revolution:

> When the American colonies began their resistance to
> English tyranny, the women—all this inherited tendency
> to freedom surging in their veins—were as active, earnest,
> determined and self-sacrificing as the men . . .[2]

These active revolutionary women saw the struggle as one that could extend the principles of democracy to all groups—including slaves and women. Gage noted that Mercy Otis Warren, Abigail Smith Adams, and Hannah Lee Corbin all "manifested deep political insight" about women's rights. During the formation of the government, Abigail Adams advised her husband John to "be more generous and favorable to [women] than your ancestors." She cautioned, "Do not put such unlimited power into the hands of the husbands," or, Abigail Adams warned, "we are determined to foment a rebellion, and will not hold ourselves bound by any laws in which we have no voice or representation."[3] "Thus did the Revolutionary Mothers urge the recognition of equal rights when the Government was in the process of formation," Gage observed.[4]

The forefathers looked with disdain on anything British as they formed their new government — until it came to forcing women into their place. Then the men looked to England for their model. The European tradition of church and law placed women in the role of property, British historian Herbert Spencer maintained. "Our laws are based on the all-sufficiency of man's rights, and society exists today for woman only in so far as she is in the keeping of some man," Gage quoted Spencer.[5]

Abigail Adams feared — accurately, it turned out — that English common law, (having been recently codified by Blackstone), would provide the basis for family law as the states solidified their laws after the revolution. It marked a decided set-back for women. Woman's "very being or legal existence was upended during marriage, or at least, incorporated or consolidated into that of the husband, under whose wing, protection and cover, she performs everything," Blackstone had written. "The two shall become one and the one is the man," the church proclaimed in canon law, and common law echoed the proclamation. Abigail Adams maintained that marriage under common law robbed woman of her rights and created conditions that encouraged men to act tyrannically.

At least one founding father joined the Revolutionary-era feminists. Tom Paine penned what was probably the first plea for equal rights published in the United States. Influenced by Mary Wollstonecraft, British women's rights advocate and author of the 1792 feminist classic, *Vindication of the Rights of Women*, Paine boldly began his 1775 essay in the *Pennsylvania Magazine* with the assertion that man is the oppressor of woman.[6]

Calls for women's rights during the Revolution, however, were ignored. Once they had cemented power, the United States revolutionaries placed women in a position of political subordination more severe even than that of the colonial period.[7]

Under the European-inspired laws adopted by each state after the revolution, a single woman might own property, earn a living, and be economically independent but, upon uttering the marriage vows, she lost control of her property and her earnings. She also gave away all rights to the children she would bear. Offspring became the "property" of the father who could give them away or grant custody to someone other than the mother, in the event of his death. With the words "I do," a woman literally gave up her identity. Legally, the woman lost her name, any right to control her own body, and to live where she might choose. A married woman could not make any contracts, sue, or be sued; she was considered dead in the law. Wife-beating was not against the law; neither was marital rape.

Women's rights

The concept of women's rights could not be easily incorporated into Euro-Christian tradition. Rather, feminism challenged the very foundation of Western institutions, Gage believed—especially that of religion.[8]

> As I look backward through history I see the church everywhere stepping upon advancing civilization, hurling woman from the plane of "natural rights" where the fact of her humanity had placed her, and through itself, and its control over the state, in the doctrine of "revealed rights" everywhere teaching an inferiority of sex; a created subordination of woman to man; making her very existence a sin; holding her accountable to a diverse code of morals from man; declaring her possessed of fewer rights in church and in state; her very entrance into heaven made dependent upon some man to come as mediator between her and the Savior it has preached, thus crushing her personal, intellectual, and spiritual freedom.[9]

"No rebellion has been of like importance with that of Woman against the tyranny of Church and State"

Matilda Joslyn Gage

Discontent came to a head for radical women's rights reformers when they realized in the late 1880s that their hard labor of forty years had not resulted in woman's equality in the church, state, work place, or family. The United States Supreme Court had ruled that the right to vote was not guaranteed to them. Still seen as the source of evil by the church because of Eve's original sin, women continued to be, as Gage called them, the "great unpaid laborers of the world," the virtual slave of the household and, in the few occupations open to them, paid only half the wages men received.

Reformers who had spent their whole lives working unsuccessfully to change woman's condition began to realize the depth of the roots of oppression. Certainly they must have had doubts. Could women's position be natural or "God-ordained," as the enemies of freedom constantly told them? Both Stanton and Gage's vision became deeper and broader as their successes failed to materialize.

Gage expressed it this way:

> During the ages, no rebellion has been of like importance with that of Woman against the tyranny of Church and State; none has had its far-reaching effects. We note its beginning; its progress will overthrow every existing form of these institutions; its end will be a regenerated world.[10]

How were these women able to see from point A, where they lived—corseted and ornamental non-persons in the eyes of the law—to point C, the "regenerated world" Gage predicted, in which all repressive institutions would be destroyed? What was point B in their lives, the real and

Corseted and ornamental non-persons in the eyes of the law.

visible alternative that drove their feminist spirit—not a utopian pipe dream but a living example of equality?

Then it dawned on me. I had been skimming over the source of their vision without even noticing it. My own stunningly deep-seated presumption of white supremacy had kept me from recognizing what these prototypical feminists kept insisting in their writings. They believed women's liberation was possible because they knew liberated women, women who possessed rights beyond their wildest imagination: Haudenosaunee women.

Gage and Stanton, major theorists of the woman suffrage movement's radical wing, became increasingly disenchanted with the inability and unwillingness of Western institutions to change and embrace the liberty of not just women, but all disfranchised groups. They looked elsewhere for their vision of the "regenerated world" and they found it—in upstate New York. They became students of the Haudenosaunee and found a cosmological world view they believed to be superior to the patriarchal, white-male-dominated view prevalent in their own nation.

Once I understood the connection, I came to realize it was everywhere—right where I hadn't seen it before. The more evidence I uncovered of this indelible Native influence on the vision of early United States feminists, the more certain I became that, previously, I had been dead wrong. Like most historians do, I had assumed that the story of feminism began with the "discovery" of America by white men, or the political revolution staged by the colonists—that there was no seed of feminism already in American soil when the first white settlers arrived. Without realizing it, I had assumed that white people had imported the germ of the idea of woman's rights and that was the end of the story. My eyes and ears, I realized, certainly needed the clearing Ray Fadden advised in his "Fourteen Strings of Purple Wampum to Writers about Indians."

A Vision of Everyday Justice

The European invasion of America resulted in genocide. That is the most important story of contact. But it is not the only one. While Europeans concentrated on "Christianizing and civilizing," relocating and slaughtering Indians, they also signed treaties, coexisted with and learned from them. Regular trade, cultural sharing, even friendship between Native Americans and EuroAmericans transformed the immigrants. Perhaps nowhere was this social interaction more evident than in the towns and villages in upstate New York where Matilda Joslyn Gage lived, Elizabeth Cady Stanton grew up, and Lucretia Mott visited. All three of these leading suffragists knew Haudenosaunee women, citizens of the Six Nations Confederacy that had established peace among themselves long before Columbus arrived at this "old" world.

Stanton, for instance, sometimes sat across from Oneida women at the dinner table in Peterboro, New York, during frequent visits to her cousin, the radical social activist Gerrit Smith.[11]   Smith's daughter (also named Elizabeth) was among the first to shed the twenty pounds

Bloomers on an American woman. Carolyn Mountpleasant,
a Seneca woman, in traditional dress.

of clothing that fashion dictated should hang from any fashionable woman's waist, usually dangerously deformed from corseting. The reform costume Elizabeth Smith adopted (named the "Bloomer" after the newspaper editor who popularized it) promised the health and comfort of the loose-fitting tunic and leggings worn by Native American friends of the two Elizabeths.

In 1853 Gage worked on a committee headed by *New York Tribune* editor Horace Greeley to document the woefully few jobs open to white women.[12] Meanwhile she knew nearby Onondaga women who farmed corn, beans, and squash—nutritionally balanced and ecologically near-perfect crops called "the Three Sisters" by the Haudenosaunee.[13]

43

Lucretia Mott and her husband, James, were members of the Indian Committee of the Philadelphia Yearly Meeting of the Society of Friends. From the 1790s on, these Quakers sent missionaries among the Seneca, educating them and supporting them against unscrupulous land speculators. During the summer of 1848 the Motts visited Cattaraugus where they witnessed women exercising equal authority in discussion and decision-making while the Seneca nation changed its governmental structure. Lucretia watched as the Native women planned the

Lucretia Mott's feminist vision was fired by her first-hand experience of women's political, spiritual, social and economic authority, in the Seneca community.

strawberry ceremony in a most non-Christian tradition of women's spiritual leadership. With her feminist vision fired by her first-hand experience of women's political, spiritual, social, and economic authority, Mott traveled from the Seneca nation to nearby Seneca Falls, where she and Stanton called the world's first woman's rights convention in July.

These suffragists regularly read newspaper accounts of everyday Iroquois activities: a condolence ceremony to mourn a chief's death and to set in place a new one; the sports scores when the Onondaga faced the Mohawks at lacrosse; a Quaker council called to ask Seneca women to leave their fields and work in the home (as the Friends said God commanded but as Mott opposed). Newspaper readers in New York also read interviews with white teachers who worked at various Indian nations testifying to the wonderful sense of freedom and safety they felt, since Indian men did not rape women. These front-page stories admonished big-city dandies to learn a thing or two from Native men's example, so that white women too could walk around any time of the day or night without fear. Rev. M. F. Trippe, long a missionary on the Tonawanda, Cattaraugus and Alleghany reservations, told a New York City reporter:

Tell the readers of the *Herald* that . . . they have a sincere respect for women—their own women as well as those of the whites. I have seen young white women going unprotected about parts of the reservations in search of botanical specimens best found there and Indian men helping them. Where else in the land can a girl be safe from insult from rude men whom she does not know?[14]

In the United States, until women's rights advocates began the painstaking task of changing state laws, a husband had the legal right to batter his wife. A North Carolina court ruled in 1864 that the State had no business meddling in wife battering cases unless "permanent injury or excessive violence" was involved. The batterer and his victim should be left alone, the court determined, "as the best mode of inducing them to make the matter up and live together as a man and wife should."[15] Suffragists knew that wife battering was not universal, living as neighbors to men of other nations whose religious, legal, social, and economic concept of women made such behavior unthinkable. To Stanton, Gage, Mott, and their feminist contemporaries, the Native American principles of everyday decency, nonviolence, and gender justice must have seemed the Promised Land.

A Vision of Power and Security

As a feminist historian, I did not at first pay attention to such references to American Indian life because, without realizing it, I accepted the stereotype that Native American women were poor, downtrodden "beasts of burden" (as they were often called in the nineteenth century). I read right past the suffragists' documentation of Native women's superior rights without seeing it.

I remembered that in the early 1970s, some feminists flirted with the idea of prehistoric matriarchies on which to pin women's egalitarian hopes. Anthropologists soon set us straight about such nonsense. The evidence just wasn't there, they said. But Paula Gunn Allen, a Laguna Pueblo/Sioux author and scholar, believed otherwise:

Beliefs, attitudes and laws such as [the Iroquois Confederation] became part of the vision of American feminists and of other human liberation movements around the world. Yet feminists too often believe that no one has ever experienced the kind of society that empowered women and made that empowerment the basis of its rules and civilization. The price the feminist community must pay because it is not aware of the recent presence of gynarchial societies on this continent is unnecessary confusion, division, and much lost time.[16]

Allen's words opened my eyes, threw into question much of what I thought I knew about the nineteenth-century woman's movement, and sent me on an entirely new course of historical discovery. The results shook the foundation of the feminist theory I had been teaching for almost twenty years.

A National Endowment for the Humanities fellowship allowed me to replicate the suffragists' research, and I tracked down Stanton's and Gage's citations, poring over books, newspapers, and journals they had read. I visited Onondaga and slowly began to know some of the women.

I sat in the kitchen of Alice Papineau—De-wa-senta—an Onondaga clan mother, on a hot summer day, drinking iced tea as she described the criteria clan mothers use to choose—and depose, if necessary—the male sachem who represents their clan in the Grand Council, a responsibility of which Stanton and Gage were well aware. But neither suffragist had explained the sachem job requirements, which De-wa-senta listed: "First, they cannot have committed a theft. Second, they cannot have committed a murder. Third, they cannot have abused a woman." And the overriding qualification: the chief needs to have shown that he can take care of a family, behave as a responsible family man, since he will be responsible for the well-being of the larger families of the clan, the nation and the confederacy—through seven generations.

There goes Congress! I think to myself, followed by a flight of fantasy: What if, in the United States, only women chose governmental representatives, and women alone had the right "to knock the horns off the head," as Stanton marveled—to oust officials if they failed to represent the needs of the people unto the seventh generation?

If I am so inspired by De-wa-senta's words today, imagine how the founding feminists felt as they beheld the Haudenosaunee world.

Elizabeth Cady Stanton was called a heretic for advocating divorce laws that would allow women to leave loveless and violent marriages. "What God hath joined together let no man put asunder," traditional Christianity intoned! She found a model in Haudenosaunee attitudes toward divorce. Stanton informed the National Council of Women in an 1891 speech, a misbehaving Iroquois husband "might at any time be ordered to pick up his blanket and budge."[17] What must it have meant to Stanton to know of such real-life domestic authority?

A Vision of Radical Respect

While early women's rights activists successfully changed some repressive laws, an ensuing backlash in the 1870s resulted in the criminalization of birth control and family planning, while custody of the children remained the exclusive right of fathers. By the 1890s, Stanton and

Family lineage traditionally was reckoned through the mothers.

her daughter, Harriet, began to envision "voluntary motherhood," the title of a speech Harriet prepared for the 1891 National Council of Women. "Motherhood is sacred—that is, voluntary motherhood," Harriet declared, "but the woman who bears unwelcome children is outraging every duty she owes the race."[18] Mother and daughter presented a revolutionary alternative to the patriarchal family, with women controlling their own bodies and having rights to the children they bore. No utopian dream, body right was a birthright of Haudenosaunee women. Family lineage traditionally was reckoned through mothers; no child was born a "bastard" (the concept didn't exist). Every child found a loving and welcome place in a mother's world, surrounded by a mother's sisters, her mother, and the men whom they married. Unmarried sons and brothers lived in this large extended family, too, until they left home to marry into another matrilineal clan.

Stanton envied how Indian women "ruled the house" and how "descent of property and children were in the female line." When called a "savage" for practicing natural childbirth, Stanton rebuked her critics by mocking their use of the word, pointing out that Indian women "do not suffer" giving birth. They "step aside the ranks, even on the march and return in a short time bearing with them the newborn child," she wrote.[19] Thus it was absurd to suppose "that only enlightened Christian women are cursed" by painful, difficult childbirth.[20]

In 1875, while serving as president of the National Woman Suffrage Association, Gage penned a series of admiring articles about the Haudenosaunee for the New York *Evening Post* in which she wrote that the "division of power between the sexes in this Indian republic was nearly equal," while the Iroquois family structure "demonstrated woman's superiority in power."[21]

For white women living in a world where marital rape was commonplace and forbidden by neither church nor state (although the Comstock Law of the 1870s outlawed discussion of it), Native women's violence-free and egalitarian home life could only have given suffragists sure knowledge that their goals could be reached. Still, they had a long way to go.

Until woman's rights advocates began to change divorce laws in the last half of the nineteenth century, women found themselves trapped in marriage, unable to leave. Women fleeing from a violent or abusive

husband could be returned to him by the police, as runaway slaves were returned to their master. Husbands could will away an unborn child, and the baby would be taken from its mother and given to its "rightful owner" when the father/guardian died. And, until married women's property acts were slowly enacted state by state throughout the nineteenth century, any money a wife earned or inherited belonged outright to her husband.

A married woman was "nameless, purseless and childless," Stanton summed up, even though she be "a woman, heiress and mother." Calling for an end to this injustice, the early suffragists were labeled hopeless dreamers for imagining a world so clearly against nature; worse, they were labeled heretics for daring to question God's divine plan. Stanton, whose major work, *The Woman's Bible*, was published in 1895, became convinced that the oppression of women was not divinely inspired at all. Gage agreed, calling the church the "bulwark" of women's oppression.

When the religious right tried to destroy religious freedom by placing God in the Constitution and prayer in public schools and by pushing a conservative political agenda in the 1890s, Stanton and Gage (Mott had died) determined to challenge the church. Their theory held that indigenous women in early history held positions of respect and authority in egalitarian and woman-centered societies that often worshiped a female deity, sometimes in combination with a male consort. This matriarchal system was overthrown, Stanton contended, when "Christianity, putting the religious weapon into man's hand, made his conquest complete."[22] While common knowledge held that Christianity and civilization meant progress for women, Stanton and Gage disagreed.

A Vision of Responsibilities

A few years ago I was invited to lecture at the annual Elizabeth Cady Stanton birthday tea in Seneca Falls along with Audrey Shenandoah, an Onondaga nation Spiritual leader. A crowd of my feminist contemporaries packed the elegant, century-old hotel, and I spoke about the rights of Haudenosaunee women. Then Audrey talked matter-of-factly about the responsibilities of clan mothers, who continue to nominate, counsel, and keep in office their clan's chief, as they always have. In the Six Nations of the Iroquois Confederacy, she explained, Haudenosaunee women have worked with the men to successfully guard their sovereign political status against persistent attempts to turn them into United States citizens. In Audrey's direct and simple telling, the social power of the Haudenosaunee women seemed almost unremarkable. "We have always had these responsibilities," she said.[23]

My feminist terminology, I suddenly realized, had revealed my cultural bias. Out of habit I had referred to women's empowerment as women's "rights." But for Haudenosaunee women who have maintained many of their traditional ways despite two centuries of white America's attempts to "civilize and Christianize" them, the concept of women's "rights" has little actual meaning. To the Haudenosaunee, it is simply their way of life. Their egalitarian relationships and their political authority are a reality that I—like my foresisters—still but dream.

Mother Earth Does Not Revolve Around the Son

I arrive, hurried, at the home of Ethel, a friend with whom I work. We have exactly an hour to meet, squeezed into a tight travel schedule. After pleasantries we get down to business, moving along at a smooth clip, and it looks as if we will finish on time when suddenly her son enters. A strapping 17-year-old, he fills the room with his presence. Ethel beams at him and hangs on his every word as he describes his teachers' deadlines, clean uniform needs, other mundane details of his day. Virginia Woolf got it right: his mother's admiring gaze reflects him twice life size. He never acknowledges my presence, she doesn't introduce us, and our work is forgotten. When finally he walks out, Ethel and I scramble to tie up loose ends, some of which still dangle as I dash out the door.

Ethel is EuroAmerican; her son stands poised to inherit the world.

A week later I sit in my friend Jeanne's living room, enjoyably chatting. I hear her 17-year-old son in the kitchen rattling pans, perhaps cooking or washing dishes. Minutes later he appears and places cups of tea in front of us without a word, his gift offered unobtrusively, his demeanor without display. I look up to thank him but he is gone, his back already turned as he repairs to the kitchen. Jeanne seems not even to notice, and our conversation continues.

Jeanne is Onondaga, a Haudenosaunee woman descended from the traditional "pagan" Iroquois—those who refused to be "Christianized" and "civilized." Her son recognizes his mother, and all women, as the center of the culture.

Such sons of such mothers belonged to our feminist foresisters' vision too. They are sons who learned from their fathers and their father's fathers to respect the sovereignty of women. They are sons of a tradition in which rape and battering of women was virtually unknown until contact with white people, a tradition in which women's rights are a birthright.

Mother Earth, Creator of Life

Haudenosaunee women were farmers. What an amazing revelation this must have been to reformers accustomed to a society where women were corseted, fashionably weak, and believed to be incapable of hard labor. Nodding their tacit approval to the prevailing social, legal and religious wisdom, most white women of means accepted their place: inside the home. Not Native women, who farmed, Gage marveled, and who did so using highly effective methods unknown to white men.

Their method of farming was entirely different from our own. In olden Iroquois tillage there was no turning the sod with a plough to which were harnessed a cow and a woman, as is seen today in Christian Germany; but the ground was literally 'tickled with a hoe' and it 'laughed with a harvest.' Corn hills three or four times larger than those seen today remained in use successive years, and when the country was first settled the appearance of those numerous little mounds created great wonder. Slightly scratched with a stick or piece of bone, maize was there planted, and but little labor attended its cultivation.[1]

Haudenosaunee women planted primarily corn, beans, and squash. Harriet Maxwell Converse (Gage's friend) explained that this nutritionally perfect combination was the staple of their diet:

The three vegetables, the corn, beans and squash were known to the Onondagas as tu-ne-ha-kwe meaning 'these we live on,' and to the Senecas as Dio-he'-ko, meaning 'our true sustenance.' It is interesting to note that among the ancient Aztecs the spirit of the maize was called Tonacayohau, She Feeds Us.[2]

Arthur C. Parker (of Seneca descendent), an acquaintance of Susan B. Anthony and an early Director of the Rochester Museum of Arts and Science (now the Rochester Museum and Science Center), explained the method of planting used by the women:

The Iroquois generally planted their squashes in the same hills with corn and some kinds of beans. Besides the land and labor saved by this custom there was a belief that these three vegetables were guarded by three inseparable spirit sisters and that the plants would not thrive apart in consequence.[3]

The spiritual harmony of the Three Sisters is also ecological. The corn stalk provides support for the beans while the beans provide nitrogen to nourish the corn. The squash covers the mound, keeping weeds out and moisture in. Eaten together, these Three Supporters constitute a nutritionally balanced diet.

Native women's honored obligation, recognized by the men, was to direct the home and the community's agriculture. Satisfying and sacred, women's work harmoniously complemented the hunting/diplomatic duties of men; both were equally valued. Within this framework of community responsibility, individual liberty flourished.

Gage knew about Mary Jemison, the white captive adopted into the Seneca nation who, when given the option of returning to the white world, chose instead to live with her Native family. Jemison's story was recorded by a Dr. Seaver and made into a popular book during Gage's childhood. Although she was eighty at the time the book was issued, Jemison still planted, tended, and harvested her corn, gathered and chopped her own wood, and fed her cattle and poultry, wearing the traditional dress. Jemison offered a detailed description of Seneca women's agricultural work:

> Our labor was not severe; and that of one year was exactly similar in almost every respect to that of the others. . . . Notwithstanding the Indian women have all the fuel and bread to procure, and the cooking to perform, their task is probably not harder than that of white women, who have

> those articles provided for them, and their cares certainly are not half as numerous, nor as great. In the summer season, we planted, tended, and harvested our corn, and generally had all of our children with us; but had not master to oversee or drive us, so that we could work as leisurely as we pleased. . . . We pursued our farming business according to the general custom of

Indian women, which is as follows: In order to expedite their business, and at the same time enjoy each other's company, they all work together in one field, or at whatever job they may have on hand. In the spring, they choose an old active squaw [sic] to be their driver and overseer, when at labor, for the ensuing year. She accepts the honor, and they consider themselves bound to obey her. . . . By this rule, they perform their labor of every kind, and every jealousy of one having done more or less than another is effectually avoided.[4]

In a newspaper report that she published on the 1875 Onondaga County Indian Fair, Gage marveled that "forty-eight kinds of beans were on exhibition." She went on to give some history of Haudenosaunee agriculture:

A Dutch history of the New Netherlands as early as 1621 speaks of the luxuriant growth of Turkey beans. Planted in hills with corn they twined around the stalks. Hendrick Hudson in 1609 saw at one place more than three shiploads of corn and beans drying, beside the crops still luxuriantly growing. It was no lack of other food that forced the Five Nations into agriculture; all kinds of game were abundant. . . . Turkeys, geese, ducks, swan, teal,

plover, pheasants, deer, bear, beaver and many other kinds of game were equally abundant, besides an infinite variety of nuts and wild fruits. But this confederacy, with its wonderful government and customs and its fixed dwelling places, had in its own steps of progress developed a science of agriculture. Corn, beans, potatoes, and plants of the gourd family, including squash and a species of pumpkin, and tobacco, were all regularly cultivated, and together with vast quantity of nuts, were stored in pits or cellars for winter use.[5]

Gage recognized the superiority of the Iroquois agricultural method. Beyond that, she believed that Haudenosaunee recognition of the spiritual, life-giving supremacy of woman's creation of food represented a higher form of civilization than her own:

Three of the five ancient feasts of the Iroquois were agricultural feasts connected with this, their great staple. The first was celebrated immediately after corn planting in May, the second, or Succotash Feast, at filling of the ears in August, and continuing for a fortnight; the third, after corn-harvest. Centuries ago was agriculture honored by this ancient people. In Christian Europe during the middle ages the agriculturist was despised; the warrior was the aristocrat of civilization. In publicly honoring agriculture as did the Ongwe Honwe three times a year, they surpassed in wisdom the men of Europe.[6]

William Beauchamp described the third spiritual ceremony Gage mentioned—the "Thanksgiving that traditionally accompanied the harvest of the Three Sisters"—as one more example of cultural borrowing. "It is noteworthy that the Indian Thanksgiving Day antedated our own," Beauchamp wrote. "It is more American than we have ever claimed."[7] Thanksgiving, it turns out, is a Native American celebration adopted by EuroAmerican settlers.

Haudenosaunee women held the sacred responsibility of creating life—from their own bodies and from the body of Mother Earth—the creation story told:

56

The Grandmother buried her daughter and planted in her grave the plants and leaves that she had clutched in her hands when she fell from the sky world. Not long after, over her daughter's head grew corn, beans and squash. These were later known as the "three sisters" and became the main life support groups for the people of the Haudenosaunee. From her heart grew the sacred tobacco which would later be used as an offering to send greetings to the Creator. At her feet grew the strawberry plants, as well as other plants that would be used as medicines to cure sickness. The earth itself was referred to as "Our Mother" by the Master of Life, because their mother had become one with the earth.[8]

Women were responsible for everything *in* the earth, while men had the care of everything *on* the earth (hunting, fishing, etc.). That was the balance. It was, ironically, the benevolent attempt to "Christianize" and "civilize" the "savage Indian" that worked to destroy the previously healthy gender balance of the Iroquois Confederacy. Missionaries insisted that woman's proper sphere was the home, and that Indian men should take up farming. When accomplished, this change not only would take away women's economic independence, leaving them as dependent as white women; it also tore at the very fabric of Native society, which held that women, producers of life, were the only appropriate group to bring life from the soil. Despite resistance, Indian land—over which women had historically been the caretakers for the nation—was often divided up among Indian men, as "heads of the family." Tribal governments, systematically changed to model after that of the United States, disfranchised women.

"It behooves us women," Stanton wrote, "to question all historians . . . who teach . . . any philosophy that lowers the status of the mothers of the race."[9] She found a suppressed history, one that elevated women. While women's work was not valued in the EuroAmerican world (if it were, it would be paid, Stanton insisted), there was nothing inherently demeaning about it, she held. To the contrary, the creative powers of woman in birthing and maintaining daily life, she came to believe, were the source of her strength. Stanton recognized the indigenous truth that agriculture grew naturally out of woman's ability to birth. In an 1891 speech to the National Council of Women she expressed this view:

> Careful historians now show that the greatest civilizing power . . . has been found in . . . motherhood. For the protection of herself and her children woman made the first home in the caves of the earth, then huts with trees in the sunshine. She made the first attempts at agriculture, raised grains, fruits, and herbs, which she learned to use in sickness. She was her own physician; all that was known of the medical art was in her hands. She domesticated the cow and the goat, and from the necessities of her children learned the use of milk. The women cultivated the arts of peace, and the sentiments of kinship, and all there was of human love and home-life. The necessities of motherhood were the real source of all the earliest attempts at civilization. Thus, instead of being a 'disability,' as unthinking writers are pleased to call it, maternity has been the all-inspiring motive or force that impelled the first steps towards a stable home and family life.[10]

Stanton recognized and valued women's work in one small way with this prayer, delivered when she was asked to bless the food at a meal:

> Heavenly father and mother, make us thankful for all the blessings of this life and make us ever mindful of the patient hands that oft in weariness spread our tables and prepare our daily food. For humanity's sake. Amen.[11]

Stanton — unlike the Christians of her day — acknowledged the divinity of woman, along with the role of women in the creation of daily life.[12] Her words expressed a sentiment somewhat similar to the Haudenosaunee Thanksgiving Address, an ancient prayer given by Iroquois elders before and after an event of importance. An oral tradition, it can take four hours to tell in its entirety. This is a contemporary Mohawk version:

> We give greetings and thanks to our Mother the Earth — she gives us that which makes us strong and healthy. We are grateful that she continues to perform her duties as she was instructed. The women and Mother Earth are

one—givers of life. We are her color, her flesh and her roots. Now our minds are one.[13]

While EuroAmericans might have lost that grounding, Native people had not. Traditionally, woman as mother and woman as creator of life were one and the same. Mother Earth was an obvious descriptive term, not a romantic metaphor. The Haudenosaunee believed that the earth would not bear unless cultivated by women. Agriculture retained its ancient spiritual connection to fertility, growth, and revival among the Haudenosaunee.

What happened to bring about the downfall of Western women from sacred creators of life-giving food to kitchen drudges? Stanton presented her theory, with which Gage agreed:

> Women and their duties became objects of hatred to the Christian missionaries and of alternate scorn and fear to pious ascetics and monks. The priestess mother became something impure, associated with the devil, and her lore an infernal incantation, her very cooking a brewing of poison, nay, her very existence a source of sin to man. Thus woman, as mother and priestess, became woman as witch. The witch trials of the Middle Ages, wherein thousands of women were condemned to the stake, were the very real traces of the contest between man and woman. Christianity putting the religious weapon into man's hand made his conquest complete.[14]

Gage documented the spiritual and practical authority Native women maintained in the field as well as in the kitchen, while acknowledging their influence on white women in both areas. "Let every eater of succotash—a 'luscious mixture' of green-corn, beans, and venison correctly called 'msickquatash'—henceforth remember to whom we are indebted for that toothsome dish." After replacing venison with pork and changing the name, "we white people speak of it as one of our national dishes," she said, when in truth, "the gustatory succotash" was given to us by Haudenosaunee women. It is not "our only culinary remembrance of the red-woman's skill in cookery," she added, "for more than one of our national dishes are ours not by invention, but by adoption from our Indian predecessors."[15]

In another article headlined, *Do You Love Corn?* Gage questioned whether the reader might "emulate Sancho Panza, and bless the man who first invented Succotash." If so, Gage was ready for a fight. "Never, Mr. Editor, you cannot deprive my sex of that glory," she challenged, for "succotash is the invention of a squaw." [sic] "White men borrowed tobacco of the Red Indian," she wrote, while "white women, more to good purpose, borrowed the art of succotash-making, and the golden pumpkin, its fit accompaniment, when in a Yankee pie."[16]

A further Gage acknowledgment of Haudenosaunee influence on cooking claimed that, "Hasty pudding was an ancient method of

Western women . . . [from] sacred creators of life-giving food to kitchen drudges.

preparing corn among the Iroquois." Her proof? Reference to *"A History of the New Netherlands*, published in Amsterdam in 1671, [which] speaks of the Indian food, called by them sappaen, and made of crushed corn boiled to a pap."[17]

Appropriately, when Hattie Burr published her *Woman Suffrage Cook Book* in 1886, Gage contributed a recipe for Indian pudding that had been handed down in her family, coming to her from her mother:

Old-Time Baked Indian Pudding

> Three pints of sweet milk, two large iron spoonfuls of yellow cornmeal, one small egg, one iron spoonful of molasses, three-fourth cup of sugar, heaped teaspoonful of ginger, level teaspoonful of cinnamon, one-third of a small nutmeg, and one-half a teacupful thick sour cream. Put half the milk over the fire with a sprinkling of salt; as soon as it comes to a boil, scatter the meal quickly and evenly in by hand. Remove immediately from the fire to a dish, stir in the cold milk, the egg well-beaten, the spices, sweetening, and sour cream. Bake three hours, having a hot oven the first hour, a moderate one the remainder of the time. Eat with sweet cream. If rightly made and rightly baked, this pudding is delicious, but four things must be remembered as requisite: First, the pudding must be thin enough to run when put in the oven, second, the egg must be small, or if large, but two-thirds used for a pudding of the above size. Third, the sour cream must not be omitted (but in case one has no cream, the same quantity of sour milk with a piece of butter the size of a small butternut can be substituted). Fourth, the baking must be especially attended to. Many a good recipe is ruined in the cooking, but if the directions are carefully followed, this pudding will be quavery when done, and if any is left, a jelly when cold. Use no sauce, but sweet cream or butter.

> Matilda Joslyn Gage, Fayetteville, N.Y.[18]

As they grew older, Stanton and Gage recognized that superficial changes in their culture and government would not bring freedom. Mirrored by surrounding nations with an ancient history of mutuality, the cutthroat world of competition in which they lived appeared flawed. "The hope of the future seems to be largely in cooperation," Gage mused.[19] Stanton concurred in the speech she delivered at her eightieth birthday party:

> My message today to our coadjutors is that we have a higher duty than the demand for suffrage. We must now, at the end of fifty years of faithful service, broaden our platform and consider the next step in progress . . . co-operation, a new principle in industrial economics. We see that the right of suffrage avails nothing for the masses in competition with the wealthy classes, and, worse still, with each other.[20]

They knew a cooperative society was possible; they had seen it.

From Subordination to Cooperation

Punished simply for being female, both religiously and legally, without rights (or even a recognized existence), the EuroAmerican wife and mother was the virtual slave of her husband. Not all men were tyrants but the law, as Lucretia Mott said, gave all men the right of tyranny. Most paid positions were closed to women and the few available ones paid no more than half the wages men received for the same work. None of this was natural or divinely inspired, said the advocates of woman's rights. They personally knew of nations where women's work stood equally valued with that of men.

Underpinnings of Western women's oppression were to be found in the Bible, Stanton and Gage believed. Genesis 3:16 consigned women to subordination to men because of the sin of Eve:

> Unto the woman he said, I will greatly multiply thy sorrow and thy conception; in sorrow thou shalt bring forth children; and thy desire *shall be* to thy husband, and he shall rule over thee.

In her *Woman's Bible*, Stanton interpreted this passage and its effect on women:

> The Bible teaches that woman brought sin and death into the world, that she precipitated the fall of the race, that she was arraigned before the judgment seat of Heaven, tried, condemned and sentenced. Marriage for her was to be a condition of bondage, maternity a period of suffering and anguish, and in silence and subjection, she was to play the role of a dependent on man's bounty . . . so long as woman accepts the position that they assign her, her emancipation is impossible.[1]

[Men] "cling to the idea of the family unit," Stanton maintained, "because on that is based the absolute power of the father over the property, children, and the civil and political rights of wives."[2] She echoed words she had written decades earlier, when she penned the

"Declaration of Sentiments" in 1848 for the first woman's rights convention in the world's history at Seneca Falls:

> He has made her, if married, in the eye of the law, civilly dead. He has taken from her all right in property, even to the wages she earns. In the covenant of marriage, she is compelled to promise obedience to her husband, he becoming, to all intents and purposes, her master—the law giving him power to deprive her of her liberty, and to administer chastisement.[3]

Violence Against Women

Elizabeth Cady Stanton was especially sensitive to the issue of divorce, publicly and consistently calling for a change in the law to allow women the right to leave loveless and dangerous marriages. She was labeled an infidel on more than one occasion for this stand, Christianity generally holding the opinion that marriage was a covenant with God which no woman had a right to break, even if her life was in danger from a violent husband. To contrast Indian-style divorce in an 1891 speech to the National Council of Women, Stanton called on the memoirs of Ashur Wright, long-time missionary (among the Seneca) whose wife, Laura, had published a dictionary of the Seneca language. Ashur Wright related:

> Usually the females ruled the house. The stores were in common; but woe to the luckless husband or lover who was too shiftless to do his share of the providing. No matter how many children, or whatever goods he might have in the house, he might at any time be ordered to pick up his blanket and budge; and after such an order it would not be healthful for him to attempt to disobey. The house would be too hot for him; and unless saved by the intercession of some aunt or grandmother he must retreat to his own clan, or go and start a new matrimonial alliance in some other.[4]

Suffragist Alice Fletcher delicately explained that "offense and injuries which can befall a woman"—marital rape and battering—when they occurred, "would be avenged and punished by the relatives under tribal law, but which have no penalty or recognition under our [United States] laws. If the Indian brother should, as of old, defend his sister, he would himself become liable to the law and suffer for his championship."[5]

> . . . the wife never becomes entirely under the control of her husband. Her kindred have a prior right, and can use that right to separate her from him or to protect her from him, should he maltreat her. The brother who would not rally to the help of his sister would become a by-word among his clan. Not only will he protect her at the risk of his life from insult and injury, but he will seek help for her when she is sick and suffering . . .[6]

Carrie S. Burnham, the legal genius of the National Woman Suffrage Association, analyzed women's position under common law. As the women had claimed in 1848, men had the right to beat their wives.

> The husband being bound to provide for his wife the necessaries of life, and being responsible for "her morals" and the good order of the household, may choose and govern the domicile, choose her associates, separate her from her relatives, restrain her religious and personal freedom, compel her to cohabit with him, correct her faults by mild means and if necessary chastise her with the same moderation as [if] she was his apprentice or child.[7]

Under common law, a husband had the right to beat his wife so long as the battering wasn't too harsh. Blackstone explained that "the husband, by the old law, might give his wife moderate correction; for, as he is to answer for her misbehaviour, he ought to have the power to control her."[8] The courts generally concurred.

In an 1864 case where a husband and wife had separated, he entered the home, "seized her by her hair, pulled her down upon the floor and held her there for some time," injuring her head and throat, the pain continuing for several months after the attack. The North Carolina Supreme Court affirmed his right to do so in an 1864 ruling that "A husband is responsible for the acts of his wife, and he is required to govern his household, and for that purpose the law permits him to use towards his wife such a degree of force as is necessary to control an unruly temper and make her behave herself, and unless some permanent injury be inflicted, or there be an excess of violence, or such a degree of cruelty as show that it is inflicted to gratify his own bad passions, the law . . . prefers to leave the parties to themselves, as the best mode of inducing them to make the matter up and live together as man and wife should."[9]

A far different fate awaited Native wife batterers, as writer Minnie Myrtle interpreted the teaching of Handsome Lake about the eternal punishment awaiting any wife batterer: "A man, who was in the habit of beating his wife, was led to the red-hot statue of a female, and requested to treat it as he had done his wife. He commenced beating it, and the sparks flew out and were continually burning him, but yet he would not consume. Thus would it be done to all who beat their wives."[10]

In the *Journal of American Folklore*, Beauchamp related an Iroquois story in which "A man who had beaten his wife cruelly upon earth, struck a red hot statue of woman. The sparks flew with every blow and burned him."[11] Minnie Myrtle attributes this story to the Code of Handsome Lake, the Haudenosaunee spiritual guide.

Fletcher was concerned about what would happen to Indian women when they became citizens, lost their rights and were treated with the same legal disrespect as white women, as she explained to the International Council of Women in 1888:

> Not only does the woman under our laws lose her independent hold on her property and herself, but there are offenses and injuries which can befall a woman which would be avenged and punished by the relatives under tribal law, but which have no penalty or recognition under our laws. If the Indian brother should, as of old, defend his sister, he would himself become liable to the law and suffer for his championship.[12]

She was referring, of course, to sexual and physical violence against women. Native men's intolerance of rape was commented upon by many eighteenth and nineteenth century Indians and non-Indian reporters alike, many of whom contended that rape didn't exist among Native nations prior to white contact.[13]

"That the woman of every Christian land fears to meet a man in a secluded place by day or night, is of itself sufficient proof of the low state of Christian morality,"[14] wrote Gage. Family friend Mary Elizabeth Beauchamp also described how, "It shows the remarkable security of living on an Indian Reservation, that a solitary woman can walk about for miles, at any hour of the day or night, in perfect safety." She elaborated, saying that Miss Remington, for example, a teacher at Onondaga, "often starts off, between eight and nine in the evening, lantern in one hand and alpenstock in the other, and a parcel of supplies strung from her shoulder, to walk for a mile or more up the hillsides." Without fear.[15] [Miss Remington, "had long been in charge of the mission house. She was adopted into the Snipe Clan of the Onondaga in 1886, and given the name "Ki-a-was-say," A new word.]

Gage is likely to have had this information. William Beauchamp's daughter-in-law dedicated her "The Battle Hymn of the Suffragists," to Matilda Joslyn Gage. Gage also wrote short stories for *The Skaneateles Democrat*—a paper edited by the father of Mary Elizabeth and William's father—in the 1850s.

Coming from a European tradition which legalized both marital rape and wife battering, it is difficult to comprehend a culture in which rape was not allowed. Living in a country where one out of three women are raped, according to current FBI statistics, it is tempting to believe—as some current scholarship would have us believe—that rape is biologically inherent. Our feminist foremothers knew better, since they knew women who lived in nations where men did not rape.

A Tuscarora Chief, Elias Johnson, wrote about the absence of rape among Haudenosaunee men in his popular 1881 history. As far as he knew, among white men, it was only the Germans who held the same respect for woman, Johnson wryly added, "until they became civilized." Maintaining that sexual violation of women was virtually unknown among all Indian men, Johnson celebrated the "marvelous" fact "that whole nations, consisting of millions, should have been so trained, religiously or domestically, that [nothing] should have tempted them from the strictest honor and the most delicate kindness."[16]

Another Tuscarora, J. N. B. Hewitt (whose publications with the Bureau of American Ethnology of the Smithsonian Institution are widely read and cited by anthropologists), substantiated Johnson's claim:

> This great regard for the person of woman was not limited to the persons of native Iroquois women, but women of alien blood and origin shared with them this respect. For example: In the face of circumstances adverse to the Iroquois, Gen. James Clinton, commanding the New York division of the Sullivan punitive expedition in 1779, with orders to disperse the hostile Iroquois and to destroy their homes, paid his enemies the high tribute of a brave soldier by writing in April, 1779, to his lieutenant, Colonel Van Schaick, then leading his troops against the Onondaga [one of the six Iroquois nations] and their villages, the following terse compliment: "Bad as these savages are, they never violate the chastity of any woman, their prisoner." And he added this significant admonition to his colonel, "It would be well to take measures to prevent a stain upon our army."[17]

A Woman's Right to Her Children

This issue of lineage had great bearing on the status[18] of women, early feminists believed. Gage wrote about the absence of a woman's right to her children in the EuroAmerican tradition:

> The slave code has always been that children shall follow the condition of the mother; hence, as the present law of marriage makes the wife the irresponsible slave of the husband—robbing her of her name, her earnings, her accountability—it consistently follows that she shall be robbed of her children. Blackstone, the chief exponent of common law, says: "A mother has no legal right or authority over her children; she is only entitled to respect and honor." The United States, governing itself by English law, inherited this with other oppressions, and it to this day holds force in most of the thirty-seven States of the Union. One or two States have by statute law placed the mother on equal basis of legal right with

the father . . . men, calling themselves Christian men, have dared to defy God's law, and to give to the father alone the sole right to the child; have dared make laws which permit the dying father of an unborn child to will it away, and to give any person he pleases to select the right to wait the advent of that child, and when the mother, at the hazard of her own life, has brought it forth, to rob her of it and to do by it as the dead father directed. What an anomaly on Justice is such a law![19]

Matilda Joslyn Gage

Gage contrasted this with the primacy of the mother-child bond among the Haudenosaunee:

> If for any cause the Iroquois husband and wife separated, the wife took with her all the property she had brought into the wigwam; the children also accompanied the mother, whose right to them was recognized as supreme.[20]

Clark, (the regional historian cited by Gage), explained that Iroquois marriage and separation required "no special ceremony, no disgrace, and each keeps their property."[21]

Amazed at the absolute authority of the mother, Gage marveled that,

> So fully to this day is descent reckoned through the mother, that blue-eyed, fair-haired children of white

fathers are numbered in the tribe and receive both from state and nation their portion of the yearly dole paid to Indian tribes. The veriest pagan among the Iroquois, the renowned and important Keeper of the Wampum, and present sole interpreter of the Belts which give the most ancient and secret history of this confederation, is Ephraim Webster, descended from a white man, who, a hundred or more years since, became affiliated through marriage with an Indian woman, as a member of the principal nation of the Iroquois, the Onondagas.[22]

Ephraim Webster, who came as a trader in 1786, lived with the Onondaga and Oneida for a quarter of a century, and was adopted into the Onondaga nation. Webster said,

> The Indians have no altercations, and that in ten years I have not heard any angry expression nor seen any degree of passion. They treated their women with respect, even tenderness. They used no ardent spirits. They settled differences amicably, raised wheat and corn in considerable quantities, and also apples.[23]

"The children always followed the *totemship of the mother*," Rose Yawger wrote in her 1893 Good Housekeeping-approved book, then explained:.

> If a Seneca brave married a Cayuga squaw [sic], the children were not Senecas, as might be supposed, but Cayugas, and even though they were born and brought up among the Senecas, they were aliens to the tribe and had to be adopted in the same ceremonious manner that strangers sometimes were. The Cayuga nation could even call on them to take arms in case of war.[24]

Minnie Myrtle, whose writing was published by the popular Appleton press in 1855, similarly wrote:

> The children are of the tribe of the mother, as are the children's children to the latest generation, and they are also of the same nation. If the mother is a Cayuga, the children

70

are Cayugas; and if a Mohawk, the children are Mohawks. If the marriage proves unhappy, the parties are allowed to separate, and each is at liberty to marry again. But the mother has the sole right to the disposal of the children. She keeps them all if she chooses, and to their father they are ever [mere] strangers.[25]

Men were mourned but, Hale wrote, "it is still harder when the woman shall die, because with her the line is lost."[26] The same sentiment prevailed among the Hurons, he explained, quoting Father Raguenea:

For a Huron killed by a Huron, thirty gifts are commonly deemed a sufficient satisfaction. For a woman forty are required, because, as they say, the women are less able to defend themselves; and moreover, they being the source whence the land is peopled, their lives should be deemed of more value to the commonwealth, and their weakness should have a stronger support in public justice.[27]

"Such was the reasoning," Hale marveled, "of these heathen barbarians. Enlightened Christendom has hardly yet advanced to the mark of these opinions."[28]

Matilda Joslyn Gage first wrote in 1875 about the "division of power between the sexes in this Indian republic" which, she contended, "was nearly equal."[29] As President of the National Woman Suffrage Association she published a series of articles on the Iroquois which were featured prominently in the *New York Evening Post* and reprinted in several other papers in the state.[30] The introduction to the series recognized the significance of this suffrage/Native American connection, stating:

Mrs. Gage, with an exhibition of ardent devotion to the cause of woman's rights which is very proper in the president of the National Woman Suffrage Association, gives prominence to the fact that in the old days when the glory of the famous confederation of savages was at its height, the power and importance of women were recognized by the allied tribes.[31]

Her writing on the superior rights of Haudenosaunee women continued, and twenty years later, Gage noted that:

> The family relation among the Iroquois demonstrated woman's superiority in power. When an Indian husband brought the products of the chase to the wigwam, his control over it ceased. In the home, the wife was absolute; the sale of the skins was regulated by her, the price was paid to her.[32]

Property Rights

EuroAmerican women lost all rights to their property when they married. Native women, men, and children all had control of their own personal property, an authority which was respected by all. Alice Fletcher talked about the property rights among the Indian women in the numerous tribes and nations she had observed, touching a sensitive nerve as she recounted this personal experience with the Omaha:

> At the present time all property is personal; the man owns his own ponies and other belongings which he has personally acquired; the woman owns her horses, dogs, and all the lodge equipments, children own their own articles, and parents do not control the possessions of their children. There is really no family property, as we use the term. A wife is as independent in the use of her possessions as is the most independent man in our midst. If she chooses to give away or sell all of her property, there is no one to gainsay her . . .[33]

> When I was living with the Indians, my hostess . . . one day gave away a very fine horse. I was surprised, for I knew there had been no family talk on the subject, so I asked: "Will your husband like to have you give the horse away?" Her eyes danced, and, breaking into a peal of laughter, she hastened to tell the story to the other women gathered in the tent, and I became the target of many merry eyes. I tried to explain how a white woman would

act, but laughter and contempt met my explanation of the white man's hold upon his wife's property.[34]

A similar story came from the pen of a French woman, Emma Borglum, who spent her 1891 honeymoon with the Dakota on the Crow Creek reservation of South Dakota, where her husband, sculptor Solon Borglum, (brother of Gutzum, the sculptor of Mt. Rushmore) was working:

> One day I showed some astonishment at seeing a young Indian woman, in the absence of her husband, give two horses to a friend. She looked at me very coldly and said: "These horses are mine." I excused myself saying that in my country a woman would consult her husband before giving such expensive presents. The woman answered proudly: "I would not be a white woman!"[35]

Minnie Myrtle wrote, "In regard to property, too, the wife retains whatever belonged to her before marriage distinct from her husband, and can dispose of it as she pleases without his consent, and if she separates from him, takes it with her, and at her death, either before or after separation, her children inherit all she possessed.[36]

It was far different for United States women under common law, which denied them property rights, as attorney Carrie S. Burnham explained:

> By marriage, the husband and wife are one person in law; that is, the legal existence of the woman is "merged in that of her husband." He is her "baron," or "lord," bound to supply her with shelter, food, clothing and medicine and is entitled to her earnings—the use and custody of her person which he may seize wherever he may find it.[37]

Stanton and Gage read early anthropologist Lewis Henry Morgan, whose study of the Iroquois also served as a basis for Frederick Engel's *On the Origins of the Family, Private Property and the State*. The Haudenosaunee thus gave a practical example and framework for the development of socialism as well as feminism.

Morgan, who left money in his will to endow a women's college at the University of Rochester, carefully explained how "not the least remarkable of their [Iroquois] institutions, was that which confined the transmission of all titles, rights and property in the female line to the exclusion of the male." To EuroAmerican men who came from a polit-ical/social heritage in which only sons could inherit, it must have been remarkable to discover "the perpetual disinheritance of the son" among the Iroquois. The Haudenosaunee principle that "the child must be the son of its mother, although not necessarily of its mother's husband" sharply contrasted with the Euro-Christian system of descent traced through the male line with legitimacy exclusively conveyed by the father.[38]

While feminists—with the support of their male allies—were wag-ing an uphill struggle to gain married women the right to control their own property and wages, Morgan pointed out that among the Iroquois:

> The rights of property, of both husband and wife, were continued distinct during the existence of the marriage relation; the wife holding, and controlling her own, the same as her husband, and in case of separation, taking it with her.[39]

In 1846, two years before the first woman's rights convention in Seneca Falls, the noted scholar Henry Schoolcraft—one of Gage's sources—had similarly written:

> Marriage, among the Iroquois, appears to be a verbal con-tract between the parties, which does not affect the rights of property. Goods, personal effects, or valuables of any kind personal or real, which were the wife's before, remain so after marriage. Should any of these be used by the husband, he is bound to restore the property or its worth in the event of separation. . . . Descent being counted by the female, may be either an original cause or effect of this unique law.[40]

While Schoolcraft's Christian-blinded eyes failed to see the spiritual foundation that rooted longhouse marriages in the hands of a supportive community, other EuroAmerican observers commented on the remark-able stability of these marriages. Economic independence seemed to be good for a marriage.

The first married woman's property law in the country was passed in Mississippi in 1839, a full nine years before New York reformed its law in 1848. Years later the Mississippi Bar Association explained how this unlikely Southern state became a leader in women's rights reform:

> Let it not be forgotten, however, whence came to us the conception. It is said, and it is no doubt true, that our first married woman's law 'in the statute of 1839' embodied and was suggested by the tribal customs of the Chickasaw Indians, who lived in our borders.[41]

The vision of economic equality in marriage spread slowly across the United States as women demanded their financial independence.

No Equality in Employment

Women's subordinate position in marriage spilled over into the world of employment as well, as the "Declaration of Sentiments" made clear at the very beginning of the woman's rights movement:

> He has monopolized nearly all the profitable employments, and from those she is permitted to follow, she receives but a scanty remuneration.
> He closes against her all the avenues to wealth and distinction, which he considers most honorable to himself. As a teacher of theology, medicine, or law, she is not known.[42]

Four years later, in her maiden speech at the third National Women's Rights Convention, held in Syracuse during 1852, Matilda Joslyn Gage pointed out the connection between lack of employment, unequal pay, and marriage:

> Because all lucrative and honorable means of support have been seized by men, . . . women have been driven to marriage as a necessity . . . or driven to a life of pollution, by the insufficiency of wages in those departments of labor which she is legitimately permitted to enter . . . men's wages are from one-half to two-thirds greater than woman's.[43]

How far removed was this life from that of Haudenosaunee women doing respected, satisfying, enjoyable work which gave them economic autonomy?

Alice Fletcher talked about her conversations with Native women who were well aware of their superior rights:

> As I have tried to explain our statutes to Indian women, I have met with but one response. They have said: "As an Indian woman I was free. I owned my home, my person, the work of my own hands, and my children could never forget me. I was better as an Indian woman than under white law."[44]

Fletcher found a similar response among Indian men:

> Men have said: "Your laws show how little your men care for their women. The wife is nothing of herself. She is worth little but to help a man to have one hundred and sixty acres." One day, sitting in the tent of an old chief, famous in war [one source says this is the Lakota medicine man, Sitting Bull], he said to me: "My young men are to lay aside their weapons; they are to take up the work of the women; they will plow the field and raise the crops; for them I see a future, but my women, they to whom we owe everything, what is there for them to do? I see nothing! You are a woman; have pity on my women when everything is taken from them."[45]

Political Outsider and Lawbreaker

The vote was the major tool that women could use in the white nation to gain their rights. They believed suffrage was their inherent right in a Republic based upon the consent of the governed. The government believed otherwise. State laws denied women suffrage and, in 1874, the United States Supreme Court ruled that they had the constitutional right to do so. Women did not achieve a recognition of their constitutional right to vote in the United States of America until the 19th Amendment to the Constitution was finally enacted in 1920, seventy-two years after the struggle began. EuroAmerican women came from an age-old tradition of political slavery, as Stanton charged in "The Declaration of Sentiments":

> The history of mankind is a history of repeated injuries and usurpations on the part of man toward woman, having in direct object the establishment of an absolute tyranny over her. He has never permitted her to exercise her inalienable right to the elective franchise. . . . Having deprived her of this first right of a citizen . . . he has oppressed her on all sides.[1]

Suffragists waged a campaign of civil disobedience during which they broke the law (by voting), refused to pay their taxes (no taxation without representation), and accused the government of failing to live up to its founding principle—a government based on the consent of the governed.

"I am a citizen of the United States and the state of New York, and demand the right to vote for the rulers and laws by which I am governed," wrote Elizabeth Cady Stanton in the *Centennial Autograph Book* at the Philadelphia Commemoration on July 4, 1876. Twenty-eight years after their first call for the vote, the suffragists of the National Woman Suffrage Association chose their words carefully. Women already had the right to vote, they argued. Were they not citizens of a Republic based on the consent of the governed? Did they not pay taxes? How wrong it would be to *ask* for a right denied them; no, they *demanded* that the federal government protect them in exercising that right.

Matilda Joslyn Gage, the movement's foremost theoretician, outlined their position in her "Woman's Rights Catechism":

Q: From whence do governments derive their just powers?

A: From the consent of the governed. (*Declaration of Independence*)

Q: Are rights granted people by governments or through constitutions?

A: No. Rights existed before governments are founded or constitutions created.

Q: Of what use then are governments and institutions?

A: To protect people in the exercise and enjoyment of their natural and fundamental rights, which existed before governments or constitutions were made. (*Declaration of Independence* and *Constitution*)

Q: What is a citizen?

A: In the United States, a citizen is a person, native or naturalized, who has the privilege of exercising the elective franchise. (*Webster*)

Q: What persons are citizens of the United States?

A: All persons born or naturalized in the United States, and subject to the jurisdiction thereof, are citizens of the United States, and of the State wherein they reside. (*14th Amendment*)

Q: What right has a citizen of the United States?

A: The right to vote . . .

Q: Are those persons who, under color of law, forbid woman the ballot, law-keepers or law-breakers?

A: They are law-breakers, acting in defiance to both National and State law, in thus refusing to women citizens the exercise of a right secured to them by the Constitution of the United States; and they render themselves liable to prosecution thereby.[2]

In this interpretation, each state was therefore a law-breaker for having laws that denied women their legal right to vote. Schooled in the anti-slavery movement, the suffragists knew that unjust laws must not be obeyed. Just as they had refused to obey the Fugitive Slave Act, they now broke the law that denied them citizenship. Gage's "catechism" laid the groundwork for a brilliant campaign of civil disobedience.

From Maryland to Washington Territory, from Fayetteville, New York, to South Newbury, Ohio, women by the hundreds, perhaps thousands, broke the law and voted in the decade after the Civil War. In Washington, D. C. over seventy women marched to the polls in a single day. In Vineland, New Jersey, 183 women attempted to vote over a four-year period. Not all the resisters were white. African American women voted in South Carolina, where the suffragist Rollin sisters wielded such influence that their home was called the unofficial Republican Party headquarters. In Michigan, Sojourner Truth, the famous former slave, joined other women at the polls.[3]

Susan B. Anthony's arrest and trial for voting in 1873 drew the nation's attention. By then, countless women throughout the country had presented themselves at the polls and none had been arrested. When the government arrested Anthony, the best-known suffragist in the United States, both Gage and Anthony understood that this would be the government's test case. Organizing a whirlwind speaking tour, they brought their cause to upstate New York villages, educating potential jurors in the county where the case would be heard. By the time Anthony went to trial, people knew that "taxation without representation" had surfaced for a second time as a burning issue in the country.

Gage described the inexperienced presiding judge as "a small-brained, pale-faced, prim-looking man," who displayed his nervousness the day of the trial, realizing that the jurors probably knew the significance of the case. "This was the first criminal case he had been called on to try since his appointment and, with remarkable forethought, he had penned his decision before hearing it," Gage wrote.[4] The judge did not allow the jury to decide the case, nor did he consult them or allow them to indicate their opinion in any way. Judge Hunt found Susan B. Anthony guilty of voting, an act expressly forbidden to women under New York State law, and fined her one hundred dollars, plus costs. Anthony refused to pay, protesting:

May it please your honor, I shall never pay a dollar of your unjust penalty. . . . And I shall earnestly and persistently continue to urge all women to the practical recognition of the old revolutionary maxim, that 'Resistance to tyranny is obedience to God.'[5]

Her defeat was simply a skirmish. The suffragists intended to win the struggle with the second part of their strategy. All around the country, women brought suit against the voter registrars who refused to accept their ballots.

Virginia Minor's case began in St. Louis when Reese Happersett, the registrar of voters, refused to place her name on the list because "she was not a 'male' citizen, but a woman," and therefore ineligible to vote in Missouri. In association with her husband Francis (married women under the common law were unable to bring suit independently of their husbands), Virginia Minor sued for damages. They lost in the Circuit Court and on appeal to the Missouri Supreme Court. Finally they carried their case to the Supreme Court, with Francis Minor acting as chief attorney. An active member of the National Woman Suffrage Association, along with his wife, Francis Minor argued what would become the landmark case for woman suffrage. The decision was unanimous. "If the courts can consider any question settled," the nine white men sitting on the Supreme Court agreed, "this is one." Chief Justice Morrison R. Waite's unanimous opinion stated, "[t]he Constitution of the United States does not confer the right of suffrage upon any one." Suffrage is not coexistent with citizenship, the Court declared, and states have the absolute right to grant or deny suffrage. Women did not have the right to vote protected in the United States of America, the Supreme Court ruled.[6]

The setback was as astonishing as it was embittering. Woman suffrage had logic on its side. All tax-paying citizens of the Republic clearly had the inherent right to give their consent to the laws under which they were ruled and the representatives who made those laws. Even Professor Walker's basic *Introduction to American Law* supported the women's rights advocates:

Women have no part or lot in the foundation or administration of the government. They cannot vote or hold office. They are required to contribute their share, by way of taxes, to the support of the Government, but are allowed no voice in its direction. They are amenable to the laws, but are allowed no share in making them. This language, when applied to males, would be the exact definition of political slavery.

The National Woman Suffrage Association convention in 1876 decided to protest against the government's treatment of women by (illegally) presenting a Declaration of Rights of Women at the official Centennial celebration, declaring:

> Whereas, The women of this nation to-day, under a government which claims to be based upon individual rights, to be "of the people, by the people, and for the people," in an infinitely greater degree are suffering all the wrongs which led to the war of the revolution; and

> Whereas, The oppression is all the more keenly felt because our masters instead of dwelling in a foreign land, are our husbands, our fathers, our brothers and our sons; therefore, Resolved, That the women of this nation, in 1876, have greater cause for discontent, rebellion and revolution, than the men of 1776.

> Resolved, . . . that, as Abigail Adams predicted, "We are determined to foment a rebellion, and will not hold ourselves bound by laws in which we have no voice or representation.[7]

The National Woman Suffrage Association had counted on the government being true to its own principles. They believed it would only be necessary to point out that the government was not living up to the founding philosophy of the country for change to occur. What they had not counted on was the sharp moral edge—backed up by the pulpit—of their opponents. "Wives, submit to your husbands," the anti's intoned, quoting St. Paul to prove that women must be subordinate to men. Religious conservatives warned that the divine order of the universe would be overturned if wives stood beside their husbands at the polling place.

Was the political subordination of women universal? If women had always been under the control of men, the suffragists would have to grudgingly admit that woman's second-class status probably revealed a divinely inspired or natural order. An exception would throw into question the universal, natural argument. The evidence of even one culture where women stood equal to men in decision-making authority would reveal the EuroAmerican practice of denying women suffrage to be an arbitrary exercise of male power.

Once again, the suffragists did not have far to look for the example they sought. Their closest cultural neighbors, Haudenosaunee women, possessed decision-making authority equally with men. Political rights were not new to these women. Their democratic government rested on decision-making by all men and women. United States women citizens had to break from their religious and political tradition in order to have a part in their government. On the other hand, woman's political participation *was* traditional for the Haudenosaunee, who believed the mutual authority of women and men was divinely inspired and necessary to maintaining the natural balance of the universe.

Ridiculed, labeled heretics, and arrested for the crime of voting, the courageous suffragists continued to believe in the rightness of their cause. They believed it was neither natural nor religiously mandated for women to be denied a voice in decisions affecting their lives and the lives of their children.

Mother of Nations

Denied a political role in their own nation, the two major theorists in the woman's rights movement, Stanton and Gage, knew and wrote about the decision-making responsibilities of women in the Six Nations. Stanton talked about how the clan mother held the authority for putting and keeping in place the chief that represented her clan:

> The women were the great power among the clan, as everywhere else. They did not hesitate, when occasion required, 'to knock off the horns,' as it was technically called, from the head of a chief and send him back to the ranks of the warriors. The original nomination of the chiefs also always rested with the women."[8]

Stanton read Lewis Henry Morgan, a Rochester lawyer known in some circles as "the father of American anthropology, who wrote *League of the Iroquois* in 1851. Morgan drew heavily on the knowledge of the Seneca, Ely S. Parker, along with the decades of personal knowledge gathered by Ashur Wright, missionary to the Seneca nation. Wright had explained women's decision-making responsibilities to Morgan in this way:

> So also if the regular heir of office should be guilty of any disqualifying conduct or should prove wanting in any respect, the old people could interfere, throw him out of line and select another in his place: and in a like manner they could depose one already a full Chief, who had been guilty of three successive disqualifying acts, and raise the next in line into his place. In the case, however, of tribal and national chiefs, it was customary for the tribe or nation to ratify their action; which they very seldom if ever failed to do. In all these matters the old women of the clans took the lead, so that it used to be said they could put up or put down whomsoever they chose, and they could approve or veto all the acts not only of the councils of their own clan, but those of the tribal and national councils also (in the latter case, in connection with the women of the other clans).

Gage described the purely democratic nature of Iroquois decision making:

> The common interests of the confederacy were arranged in councils, each sex holding one of its own, although the women took the initiative in suggestion, orators of their own sex presenting their views to the council of men.[9]

Voting is not a concept that makes an easy cross-cultural transfer. The United States government takes the form of a representative democracy, with each citizen having a vote (initially African American men and all women were not allowed to participate, of course), and the majority rules. Among the Haudenosaunee, decisions are made by consensus and everyone must agree. It has been that way since the founding of the

Confederacy, long before Europeans arrived on this continent. Voting, per se, does not exist. Rather, people speak and listen to one another, carefully considering ideas, until they are all of one mind. There is a balance of responsibilities between men and women that allows consensus to work.

This reality presented a startling contrast to the "liberty and justice for all" nation which denied women — despite their continuous protest — any part in their own government. Among the Six Nations of the Iroquois Confederacy, as Morgan explained, the intricate system of female lineage "lay at the foundation of their political as well as social organization."[10] Hewitt described what a family-based government looked like:

> The ohwachira [matrilineal family] which in their own right possessed official titles of hereditary chiefships, and lesser officials, filled these offices by nomination by the suffrages of the mothers and adult girls in them. The federal chief who represented the ohwachira in the tribal council and also in the federal council [the Iroquois League] and the chief warriors as well, were chosen in this manner, usually with the advice of the warriors of the ohwachira. The woman trustee chief, [clan mother] the highest official known to Iroquois polity, was also nominated and confirmed in this manner. She was the executive officer of the ohwachira and was chosen because of exceptional ability and purity of character; she had a seat in the federal council in addition to her position as a trustee of her ohwachira, and so had a somewhat higher standing and authority than had the male federal chief.[11]

The Haudenosaunee world view is based on keeping everything in balance. Women and men each have responsibilities they must carry out to maintain this balance. The clan mother heads the entire extended family that makes up a clan. Since the ancient founding of the League of the Haudenosaunee, which Barbara Mann and Jerry Fields have dated at 1142 C.E.,[12] each clan mother has the responsibility for carrying out the process by which the women of her clan select a male chief. The clan mother also has the duty of deposing the chief if he fails to perform his official duties. The man cannot become a chief or remain a chief if he

84

Women's Nominating Wampum Belt

commits rape, which is considered one of the three major crimes—theft and murder are the other two.

Balance also requires that everyone in the nation have a voice, and decision-making is achieved by consensus in public councils. All questions, including the making of treaties and deciding on issues of war and peace, have always required the approval of both women and men. This ancient democratic government continues to this day, with clan mothers still choosing the chiefs. The women's nominating wampum belt records this law of the Confederacy of the original Five Nations:

> We give and assign the sacred chieftainship titles and the
> soil of our land to all of our Mothers, the Women of the
> Five Nations, and they shall be the proprietors of the
> same."[13]

Arthur C. Parker describes the critical female role in the formation of the confederacy which resulted in women having responsibility for holding the chieftainship titles:

> Likewise, in the wampum codes of the Six Nations of the
> Iroquois, we are told that both Hiawatha, the Onondaga

and the Peacemaker, a Wyandot, made their journeys to the tribes with the 'Great Mother,' Ji-gon-sa-seh, the Kakwah, and consulted her in every important detail. Without the approval of their 'Mother of Nations' and her sanction of Hiawatha's plans, the integrity of the principles of the confederacy of the Five Nations would have been assailed. But Ji-gon-sa-seh, who was regarded as a descendant of the first Ye-go-wa-neh, the woman who was the mother of all the first Ongwe was sacred to her people, for her word was law and her sanction was necessary in all political measures of inter-tribal importance.[14]

The decision to place women in the highest position of governmental, as well as social, authority, was thoughtfully made by the founding mothers and fathers of the Six Nations Confederacy. Hewitt explained:

> The astute founders of the league had made the experiment of entrusting their government to a representative body of men and women chosen by the mothers of the community; they did not entrust it to a hereditary body, nor to a purely democratic body, nor even to a body of religious leaders. The founders of the league adopted this principle and with wise adjustments made it the underlying principle of the league institutions.[15]

Even when the Seneca, in a desperate attempt to maintain their land abandoned their traditional system and emulated the United States constitutional form of government—as had the Cherokee—the women still maintained their traditional authority over the land, as Minnie Myrtle wrote in 1855:

> The legislative powers of the nation are vested in a Council of eighteen, chosen by the universal suffrages of the nation; but no treaty is to be binding, until it is ratified by three-fourths of all the voters, and *three-fourths of all the mothers of the nation!*[16] So there was peace instead of war, as there would often be if the voice of woman could be heard! And though the Senecas, in revising their laws and customs, have in a measure acceded to the civilized barbarism of treating the opinions of women with contempt,

where their interest is equal, they still cannot sign a treaty without the consent of *two thirds of the mothers*![17]

Myrtle also described the political authority women held in the traditional way:

> The emblem of power worn by the Sachem [chief] was a *deer's antlers*, and if in any instance the women disapproved of the election or acts of a Sachem, they had the power to *remove his horns* and return him to private life. Their officers or *runners* from council to council were chosen by themselves and denominated *women's men*, and by these their interests were always fully represented. If at any time they wished any subject considered, by means of their runners, they called a council in their clan; if it was a matter of more general interest there was a council of the nation, and if the opinions of the women or Sachems of other nations were necessary, a grand council was called as readily to attend to them as to the interests of men. Thus a way was provided for them to have *a voice* in the affairs of the nation, without endangering their *womanly reserve* or subjecting them to the masculine reproach of publicity, or a desire to assume the offices and powers of men![18]

The emblem of power worn by the Sachem is a deer's antlers.

Gage's first-hand knowledge of Haudenosaunee political structure came through her friendship with Harriet Maxwell Converse, known widely for her creation of cultural bridges between Native and EuroAmerican people. Converse, in turn, introduced Gage to Mohawk friends, who decided to give Gage an honorary adoption into their clan, the Wolf. Gage's Mohawk sister told her that "this name would admit me to the *Council of Matrons*, where a vote would be taken, as to my having a voice in the chieftainship," Gage wrote.[19] This was in 1893, the same year Gage was arrested for voting in a school board election in Onondaga County, New York. While offered the possibility of decision-making rights in her adopted nation, Gage was arrested for voting in her own community! Would this not have profoundly affected her vision?

War and Peace and Land

Iroquois women were involved in all decisions of governmental policy, from the local to the federal level, as white reformers well knew. This extended to issues of war and peace. Timothy Dwight, writing in 1822, stated that if the warriors wanted to go to war, they needed the consent of the women:

> If the women opposed the enterprise the warriors always gave it up, because the opposition of such a female council to any public undertaking was regarded as a bad omen.[20]

French observers Lafitau and Charlevoix 200 years earlier had stated that the "chief matrons" who were the "principal women" could order the warriors to cease and desist from war.[21] Beyond being a "bad omen," since the women were responsible for providing the food and clothing the warriors needed, there was an economic basis to their authority. If the women withheld food and moccasins, the warriors stayed home. According to Gage:

> Although it was a confederation of warriors, owing its permanence and its growth to prowess in arms, yet its women exercised controlling power in peace and war, forbidding at will its young braves to enter battle, and often determining its terms of peace.[22] . . . Sir William Johnston mentions an instance of Mohawk squaws [sic] forbidding the war-path to young braves.[23]

Another famous instance occurred when the Seneca had reached an impasse in their dealings with the United States which threatened to lead to war. The women intervened and addressed the U. S. government's representative. Minnie Myrtle described it:

> In the year 1791, when Washington wished to secure the neutrality of the Six Nations, a deputation was sent to treat with them, but was not favorably received, as many of the young Chiefs were for war and sided with the British. The women, as is usual, preferred peace, and argued that the land was theirs, for they cultivated and took care of it, and, therefore, had a right to speak concerning the use that should be made of its products. They demanded to be heard on this occasion, and addressed the deputation first themselves in the following words: "Brother:—The Great Ruler has spared us until a new day to talk together; for since you came here from General Washington, you and our uncles the Sachems have been counselling together. Moreover, your sisters, the women, have taken the same into great consideration, because you and our Sachems have said so much about it. Now, that is the reason we have come to say something to you, and to tell you that the Great Ruler hath preserved you, and that you ought to hear and listen to what we, women, shall speak, as well as the Sachems; *for we are the owners of this land*, AND IT IS OURS! It is we that plant it for our and their use. Hear us, therefore, for we speak things that concern us and our children; and you must not think hard of us while our men shall say more to you, for we have told them.

The women then designated Red Jacket as their speaker, who represented them in this way:

> BROTHERS FROM PENNSYLVANIA:—You that are sent from General Washington, and by the thirteen fires; you have been sitting side by side with us every day, and the Great Ruler has appointed us another pleasant day to meet again.

We are left to answer for our women, who are to conclude
what ought to be done by both Sachems and warriors.

Red Jacket — Sagoyawatha

NOW LISTEN BROTHERS:—You know it has been the request of our head warriors, that we are left to answer for our women, who are to conclude what ought to be done by both Sachems and warriors. So hear what is their conclusion. The business you come on is very troublesome, and we have been a long time considering it; and now the elders of our women have said that our Sachems and warriors must help you, for the good of them and their children, and you tell us the Americans are strong for peace.[24]

In treaty negotiations with the Six Nations of the Iroquois Confederacy, representatives of the newly created United States government had to deal directly and indirectly with Haudenosaunee women, a fact well-known in the nineteenth-century to those who read the wide selection of popular books on the Iroquois. Women's political power, combined with their responsibility for the land, gave them authority in the making of treaties. According to Gage:

No sale of lands was valid without consent of the [women] and among the State Archives at Albany, New York, treaties are preserved signed by the "Sachems and Principal Women of the Six Nations."[25]

Fletcher also described women's involvement in treaty negotiations:

In olden times the women claimed the land. In the early treaties and negotiations for the sale of land, the women had their voice, and the famous Chief Cornplanter was obliged to retract one of his bargains because the women forbade, they being the land-holders, and not the men. With the century, our custom of ignoring women in public transactions has had its reflex influence upon Indian custom.[26]

William Stone, writing of this story in 1841, cautioned his readers:

Very erroneous opinions are generally entertained among civilized people, in regard to the consideration in which their women are held by the American Indians, and the degree of influence they exercise among them . . . although the respect with which they are treated by their lords is not as refined and spiritualized as among the cavaliers in the days of chivalry, still it may safely be averred that in the adjustment of weighty and difficult matters, no other people are in the habit of treating the opinions of their women with greater deference than the America Indians.[27]

Stone went on to explain:

It is one of the peculiar features of Indian polity that their lands belong to the warriors who defend, and the women who till them, and who, moreover, are the mothers of the warriors. And although the sachems, as civil magistrates, have ordinarily the power of negotiating treaties, yet whenever the question of a sale of land is the subject of a negotiation, if both the warriors and women become dissatisfied with the course the sachems are pursuing, they have the right to interpose and take the subject out of their hands.[28]

Also often cited were instances in which Iroquois women, through their male representatives, had addressed the U.S. government. One example was the last general council held by the United States with the Iroquois Confederacy at Canandaigua in 1794. There, Haudenosaunee women countered a prayer offered by Jemima Wilkinson, the itinerant preacher, who called on the Indians to repent. The Iroquois women responded through their representative that "the white people had pressed and squeezed them together, until it gave them great pain at their hearts, and they thought the white people ought to give back all the lands they had taken from them." They, in turn, called on the white people "to repent and wrong the Indians no more."[29]

Women's Rights Support by Haudenosaunee Men

The injustice of women's lack of political freedom in the United States was recognized by Haudenosaunee men. Dr. Peter Wilson, a Cayuga chief, addressed the New York Historical Society in 1866, encouraging United States men to give everyone the vote, "even the women, as in his

92

nation," according to a newspaper report read by Gage.[30]

Arthur C. Parker reminded non-Native readers in 1909:

> Does the modern American woman [who] is a petitioner
> before man, pleading for her political rights, ever stop to
> consider that the red woman that lived in New York state
> five hundred years ago, had far more political rights and
> enjoyed a much wider liberty than the twentieth century
> woman of civilization?[31]

Just as Iroquois men recognized the great injustice being done to
United States women, Gage made the connection between the women's
struggle for rights and the one being waged by Native nations, writing in
her newspaper in 1878:

> That the Indians have been oppressed, —are now, is true,
> but the United States has treaties with them, recognizing
> them as distinct political communities, and duty towards
> them demands not an enforced citizenship but a faithful
> living up to its obligations on the part of the
> Government.[32]

Gage drew on the parallel struggles for political self-determination of
Native nations and United States women in a resolution proposed and
adopted by the National Woman Suffrage Association at their 1879 convention:

> Resolved. That the policy of this government in appoint-
> ing agents to educate and civilize the Indians, to obtain
> calico dresses for squaws [sic] and aprons for papooses
> and a comfortable salary for their own pockets out of
> money justly due the Indian tribes, is in harmony with
> man's treatment of woman in appropriating her property,
> talents, time and labors, and using the proceeds as he
> pleases in the name of protection."[33]

Of all the amazing information about Iroquois women's political
authority, Gage was most impressed by the influence the Haudenosaunee
had on the Founding Fathers. The United States government, she realized,
was patterned after the Iroquois Confederacy:

But the most notable fact connected with woman's participation in governmental affairs among the Iroquois is the
statement of Hon. George Bancroft that the form of government of the United States was borrowed from that of
the Six Nations. Thus to the Matriarchate or Mother-rule
is the modern world indebted for its first conception of
inherent rights, natural equality of condition, and the
establishment of a civilized government upon this basis."[34]

Arthur Parker wanted white women to recognize how they were
influenced by their Haudenosaunee sisters in their struggle for a place in
the United States government:

Today as woman stands the advocate and petitioner of her
own cause, should she not offer an oblation of gratitude to
the memory of the Iroquois Indian, who called the earth
his 'first mother' and through his savage sense of justice
gave to the mothers of his race, their rights: maternal,
civil, religious, social and political."[35]

Gage recognized this—and more. "Under their women," she wrote,
"the science of government reached the highest form known to the
world."[36]

Congresswoman Louise Slaughter gave that long overdue thank you
to Haudenosaunee women at the opening ceremonies of Celebrate '98 in
Seneca Falls, New York, on July 16, 1998. In acknowledgment of the
Native practice of equality of rights, which modeled and laid a path for
the early women's rights movement, the 150th anniversary commemoration of the first woman's rights convention began with the First Words,
the Thanksgiving Address, spoken in Mohawk by Wolf Clan member
Judy Swamp on behalf of the people of the world. Thus history was
made in the course of celebrating history, for the opening words were
spoken by a member of the clan which adopted Matilda Joslyn Gage in
1893. And so has the woman's movement come full circle.

Sisters in Spirit with Haudenosaunee women, EuroAmerican suffragists looked forward to a future inspired by the knowledge that woman's
rights was a lived reality, not just a dream. As Stanton said in an 1891
speech:

Every woman present must have a new sense of dignity and self-respect, feeling that our mothers, during some periods in the long past, have been the ruling power, and that they used that power for the best interests of humanity. As history is said to repeat itself, we have every reason to believe that our turn will come again . . .[37]

Afterword

Tehanetorens (Ray Fadden), who founded the Akwesasne Mohawk Counselor Organization, is "recognized as an outstanding figure in Six Nations culture and history,"[1] according to Julius Cook in his biographical sketch of Ray in *New Voices from the Longhouse: an Anthology of Contemporary Iroquois Writing*.

I sent Ray a copy of Matilda Joslyn Gage's 1893 classic, *Woman, Church and State* in the 1980s and he sent me back some extraordinarily insightful comments, comparing the church's role in the oppression of women with that of Indians.

"Male bishops denounced new female bishop" heralds an undated and yellowing Associated Press clip in my files. "From Syracuse paper last week" Ray Fadden's red pen identified it before he sent it off to me. Bishops of six of the 99 dioceses of the Episcopal Church greeted the election of the first female bishop with the declaration that the Anglican faith would be "irreparably compromised" with Rev. Barbara Harris' consecration, and further they could not "accept the validity of ordinations or confirmations she administers," the article stated. Catholic threats greeted the news as well, with J. Francis Stafford, head of the Roman Catholic bishops' ecumenical affairs committee, warning that "a woman's becoming an Anglican bishop would hinder the 'process of reconciliation' with Roman Catholicism." Ray summed up his reaction in one red word: "DISGUSTING."

This is the letter Ray wrote when he finished reading *Woman, Church and State*:

Onchiota, N.Y.
Nov. 23, 1988

Sally R. Wagner
Dear Friend,
Pardon the delay in answering your message which reached me some time ago. Thanks for the wonderful book WOMEN which I have been reading every evening and which I have finally finished reading, also for the very good articles that you have written about the Iroquois

Confederacy, all of them SUPER and hit the nail right on the head. I am passing that book around for others to see—read—and think about. I wish that every person in the country would read that book, it is great, believe me. The truth about the various Christian religions I have always suspicioned and wondered about, but the book proves what I have always believed.

For the life of me I can't see how the white man from Europe, with that Bible under his arm, can teach that equality and democracy came from their country. Those strange laws where a noble sleeps with a peasants wife the first nights when the peasant is married. That strange belief that women invented evil. That belief that the royal families are immune from murder, rape, thievery, and every other crime and cannot be taken to court for those crimes. That strange belief that God speaks through the king's mouth (now it is the Pope) so you have to do everything he says, because it is God who is speaking. That strange belief that when one noble is fighting another noble on the other side and if one of the serfs accidentally or deliberately kills a member of the royalty on the other side, that he is immediately killed by his own side because it is a sin to kill any member of a royal family, even if he is an enemy, and on and on.

How can you say that people with these strange beliefs had any kind of a democracy, and what is amazing is that these beliefs were taught by the Christian church. The Christian church has done a lot of harm around the world. They were against Democracy and still are, they were against women having a voice, against education for the common people, against using a drug to stop pain when you are having a painful operation, against vaccination for smallpox, and against just about every move toward true freedom. It is about time that the people of the world wake up and do their own thinking.

If that bird (apologize to the bird) in Washington and those fat money-loving leaders in Congress, if women took their place, I'll bet that we would not have wars because what woman in her right mind would send her husband, her father, her son half way around the world to get his head blown off for an oil company, a chemical company, a mining company, or some other giant company or corporation. If there were more women in the high seats of government we would not have wars. Women are the natural leaders when it comes to thinking of the future and the welfare of their children. Look at history. Man rushes into things of that nature, wars and their evil. He has always been drunk with power. He never learns but he believes that might makes right. Go back in history and it has always been that way. He keeps talking about peace, but his every action is and always has been for power, war and the evil that goes with it. It was bad enough when war weapons were guns but now they have weapons that might destroy the earth and every living thing and when you give this power to power-drunk idiots, you have a dangerous situation.

Whoever the Creator is, and it could well be a Woman, gave every people their language, religion and way of life. When these hypocrites traveled around the world, having the nerve that they spoke for God, the Great Spirit, I say that they were working against God, whoever He, She, It, They were or are. It is like taking an Eagle, putting him in a cage and trying to make a chicken out of the Eagle. You cannot do it and you work against God. Nobody knows who God is and it could be a Woman. Life comes from a female, not a male.

Christian beliefs are that you are supposed to conquer the earth or the "Wilderness." Indians did not try to do this. They studied the Earth and the various creatures that live on the earth. Study nature. It is always the female who shows compassion. You have a female cat and a male cat. The female will kill twice as many mice as the male. The robin sings near the nest, but if an enemy comes, it is the female who gives her life for her little ones. A cripple or hurt animal is in the road. A man will try to kill it, run it down. A woman will stop her car and try to help it. She shows compassion. Among the animal and bird People, the female has always been the wiser, looking to the future. It has always been that way, and man is an animal also.

I am not much of a letter writer, am old and type by the finger method, hit and often miss. Thanks for your good work, and keep it up. I close this message for now. May it find you well and strong. May Sakoiatison, Creator, watch over your home, is my wish.

A Friend,

Tehanetorens or Ray Fadden

98

Endnotes

Who Gets To Be Part of History?

1. Ray Fadden, "Fourteen Strings of Purple Wampum to Writers about Indians," in *New Voices from the Longhouse: an Anthology of Contemporary Iroquois Writing*, [ed.] by Joseph Bruchac. Greenfield Center, New York: The Greenfield Review Press, 1989, pp. 97-98.

2. Ray, who founded the Akwesasne Mohawk Counselor Organization, is "recognized as an outstanding figure in Six Nations culture and history," according to Julius Cook in his biographical sketch of Ray in *New Voices from the Longhouse: an Anthology of Contemporary Iroquois Writing*, p. 96.

3. Matilda Joslyn Gage, "Letter to the Editor," *Lucifer the Lightbearer*, 21 February 1890.

4. Speech, quoted in *Lucifer the Light Bearer*, 13 March 1885.

5. Matilda Joslyn Gage, *Woman, Church and State*, Chicago: Charles Kerr, 1893; reprint ed., Aberdeen, South Dakota: Sky Carrier Press, 1998, p. 145.

6. Elizabeth Cady Stanton to Sara Underwood, 19 October 1889 and 9 May 1889, Stanton Papers, Special Collections, Vassar College Libraries, Poughkeepsie, New York.

7. Matilda Joslyn Gage, "Woman in the Early Christian Church," *Report of the International Council of Women, Assembled by the National Woman Suffrage Association . . . 1888.* Washington, D.C.: Rufus H. Darby, 1888, p. 401.

8. Lois Banner, *Elizabeth Cady Stanton: A Radical for Woman's Rights*. Boston: Little Brown and Company, 1980, p. 145.

9. Elizabeth Cady Stanton, Susan B. Anthony and Matilda Joslyn Gage, *History of Woman Suffrage* Vol. 1, New York: Fowler and Wells, 1881; reprint ed., Salem New Hampshire: Ayer Company Publishers, Inc., 1985, p. 604.

10. Elizabeth Cady Stanton to Lucretia Mott, 19 July 1876, quoted in Stanton, Anthony and Gage, *History of Woman Suffrage* Vol. 3, Rochester: Susan B. Anthony, 1886; reprint ed., Salem New Hampshire: Ayer Company Publishers, Inc., 1985, pp. 45-47.

11. Gage, *Woman, Church And State*, p. 76.

12. *The* (Washington, D.C.) *Alpha*, May 1880, p. 6.

13. Elizabeth Cady Stanton, "Elizabeth Cady Stanton on Socialism." Chicago: The Progressive Woman, 1898.

14. Gage, *Woman, Church And State*, p. 253.

15. Ibid., 257.

16. Elizabeth Cady Stanton, *The Revolution* (New York), 14 January 1869.

₁7. Matilda Joslyn Gage, *Speech of Mrs. M.E.J. Gage at the Woman's Rights Convention held at Syracuse, September 1852*. Woman's Rights Tract No. 7. Syracuse: Master's Print, 1852.

18. Gage, "The Remnant of the Five Nations: Woman's Rights Among the Indians." *The* (New York) *Evening Post*, 24 September, 1875. Scrapbook of Gage's Published Newspaper Articles, Matilda Joslyn Gage Collection, Schlesinger Library, Radcliffe College, Cambridge, Mass.

19. "A Notable Position." Unidentified newspaper clipping, July 1896, Iroquois collection, Onondaga Historical Association, Syracuse, N.Y.

20. Ibid.

21. Turner, Orsamus, *Pioneer History of the Account of the Holland Purchase of Western New York*. Buffalo: Geo. H. Derby and Co., 1850.

22. "The Onondaga Indians." *The* (New York) *Evening Post*, 3 November, 1875. Scrapbook of Gage's Published Newspaper Articles, Matilda Joslyn Gage Collection, Schlesinger Library, Radcliffe College, Cambridge, Mass.

23. Minnie Myrtle, *The Iroquois; or, The Bright Side of Indian Character*, New York: D. Appleton and Company, 1855, p. 299.

24. Ibid, pp. 24-25, 65-66.

25. *Onondaga Standard*, 11 October 1890. Iroquois Clipping File, Onondaga Historical Association, Syracuse, New York.

Haudenosaunee Women: An Inspiration To Early Feminists

1. Gage, "The Remnant of the Five Nations: Woman's Rights Among the Indians."

2. Gage, *Woman, Church and State*, p. 5.

3. Matilda Joslyn Gage editorial, "Indian Citizenship," *National Citizen and Ballot Box*, May 1878.

4. Matilda Joslyn Gage to "My dear Helen," 11 December 1893, Gage Collection, Schlesinger Library, Radcliffe College.

5. "Capt. Oren Tyler," 1906. Seneca Falls Historical Society Papers, Seneca Falls, New York.

6. *Free Enquirer*, Vol. 2, No. 1, p. 406; Vol. 2, No. 3, pp. 200-201; Vol. 2, No. 4, pp. 293-294; Vol. 2, No. 5, pp. 155, 264; Vol. 3, No. 1, p. 112; Robert Dale Owen, "The Moral Physiology" in *Birth Control and Morality in Nineteenth Century America: Two Discussions*. New York: Arno Press, 1972, p. 46.

7. Harriet S. Caswell, *Our life Among The Iroquois Indians*. Boston and Chicago: Congregational Sunday-School and Publishing Society, 1892. pp. 29-30.

8. Harriet Phillips Eaton, letters to Matilda Joslyn Gage, 1890s. Matilda Joslyn Gage Collection, Schlesinger Library, Radcliffe College, Cambridge, Mass.

9. *New York Herald*, 5 November 1905. Iroquois collection, Onondaga Historical Association, Syracuse, N.Y.

10. *Onondaga Standard*, 8 January 1946. Iroquois collection, Onondaga Historical Association, Syracuse, N.Y.

11. *Marcellus Observer*, 8 July 1949. Iroquois collection, Onondaga Historical Association, Syracuse, N.Y.

12. Unidentified newspaper clipping, 17 April 1893, Iroquois collection, Onondaga Historical Association, Syracuse, N.Y.

13. Erminnie Smith, *Myths of the Iroquois*. U. S. Bureau of American Ethnology, 2nd Annual Report, 1880-1881. Washington, D.C.:1883; reprint ed. Ohsweken, Ontario, Canada: Iroqrafts, 1994.

14. Mary Elizabeth Beauchamp, "Letter to the Editor," *Skaneateles Democrat*, 10 April 1883, Beauchamp File, Onondaga Historical Association, Syracuse, New York. In William Beauchamp's papers in the Onondaga County Library, he has listed a number of articles Mary Elizabeth wrote for the *Baldwinsville Gazette* as well as the *Skaneateles Democrat*. William Beauchamp writes, "She wrote many poems, stories and letters. I have also a typewritten Quaker story by her, unpublished and her last work. She wrote a great deal for the *Family* (Troy, N.Y.), *Journal*, *Gospel Messenger*, *Churchman*, *Living Church* and local papers."

15. Caswell, Life, p. 289; William M. Beauchamp, *Iroquois Folk Lore Gathered from the Six Nations of New York*. Empire State Historical Publication 31, n.d.; reprint ed. Port Washington, N.Y.: Ira J. Friedman Division, Kennikat Press, n.d., p. 7.

16. The Iroquois collection in the Onondaga Historical Association in Syracuse, N.Y., is an extraordinarily rich resource of 100 years of articles clipped from Onondaga County newspapers.

The Untold Story

1. Matilda Joslyn Gage, "Preceding Causes," in Stanton, Anthony and Gage, *History of Woman Suffrage* Vol. 1, p. 29.

2. Stanton, Anthony and Gage, *History of Woman Suffrage* Vol. 1, p. 31.

3. Abigail Adams letter of 31 March 1776, quoted, among other sources, in Stanton, Anthony and Gage, *History of Woman Suffrage* Vol. 3, pp. 19-20 and Eleanor Flexner, Century of Struggle, New York: Atheneum, 1974, p. 15. Abigail Adams letter of 7 May 1776 quoted in *Should Women Vote? Important Affirmative Authority*, N.p.: Equal Rights Association, n.d., p. 4. Original source was an edition of their correspondence (*Familiar Letters of John Adams and His Wife, Abigail Adams, During the Revolution*), published during 1876 by

their grandson, Charles Francis Adams, and obviously read by the suffragists, who cited it in their 1876 protest.

4. Stanton, Anthony and Gage, *History of Woman Suffrage* Vol. 1, p. 33.

5. Herbert Spencer, *Descriptive Sociology of England*. London: Williams and Morgate, 1873. Described by Gage as the "epitome of English history" in *History of Woman Suffrage* Vol. 1, p. 26.

6. Tom Paine, "Occasional Letter on the Female Sex," *Pennsylvania Magazine*, March 1775.

7. See Chapter 4 in Sally Roesch Wagner, *A Time of Protest: Suffragists Challenge The Republic 1870-1887*, Aberdeen, S.Dak.: Sky Carrier Press, 1992.

8. For an excellent theoretical analysis of the "eurocentric notion," see Jose Barreiro, "Challenging the Eurocentric Notion" in *Indian Roots of American Democracy*. Ithaca, N.Y.: Northeast Indian Quarterly, 1988, pp. xii-xvi.

9. Gage, *Woman, Church and State*, p. 324.

10. Gage, *Woman, Church and State*, p. 324.

11. Henry B. Stanton, *Random Recollections*. New York: Macgowan and Slipper, 1886, p. 94. Elizabeth Cady Stanton's husband Henry describes the frequent presence of Oneidas during their visits to Peterboro.

12. "Equal pay for equal work" was a major theme of the New York state woman's rights convention held in Rochester during 1853. "Why should not woman's work be paid for according to the quality of the work done, and not the sex of the worker?" the convention call asked. Greeley chaired the five-member Committee on Industry on which Gage served. Stanton, Anthony and Gage, *History of Woman Suffrage* Vol. 1, pp. 577, 589.

13. John Vivian in "the Three Sisters: the nutritional balancing act of the Americas" (*Mother Earth News*, February/March 2001, p. 50) describes the "complete nutritive punch" of these three plants. A "nearly ideal foundation food," corn lacks only riboflavin and niacin, along with two essential amino acids—lysine and tryptophane—all supplied by beans. Carbohydrate-rich squash contributes quality vegetable fats the other two lack, along with vitamin A.

14. Harriet Maxwell Converse, "New York's Indians," *New York Herald*, 2 February n.d. Writings of H. M. Converse and Miscellaneous Scrapbook of Ely S. Parker, p. 109. New York State Archives, Albany, New York.

15. R. Emerson and Russell P. Dobash, "Wives: The 'Appropriate' Victims of Marital Violence," *Victimology: An International Journal* Vol. 2, 1977-78, pp. 430-431.

16. Paula Gunn Allen, *The Sacred Hoop: Recovering the Feminine in American Indian Traditions*. Boston: Beacon Press, 1986, pp. 213-214.

17. Elizabeth Cady Stanton, "The Matriarchate or Mother-Age," National Council of Women of the United States. Rachel Foster Avery (ed.), *Transactions of the National Council Women of the United States, Assembled in Washington,*

D.C. February 22 to 25, 1891. Philadelphia, Pa.: 1891, pp. 218-227. Stanton-Anthony Papers 28: 1013-1017. Also published in *The National Bulletin* Vol. 1, February 1891.

18. Harriet Stanton Blatch, "Voluntary Motherhood." *The National Bulletin* Vol. 1, No. 5, February 1891, pp. 7-12.

19. Elizabeth Cady Stanton, "If You Would be Vigorous and Healthy" in M. L. Holbrook, M.D., "Parturition Without Pain," appendix to George H. Napheys, *The Physical Life of Woman: Advice to the Maiden, Wife and Mother.* New York: M.A. Donohue and Company, 1927, pp. 365-366.

20. Stanton, "The Matriarchate or Mother-Age."

21. Gage, "The Remnant of the Five Nations: Woman's Rights Among the Indians."

22. Stanton, "The Matriarchate or Mother-Age."

23. Audrey Shenandoah, Speech at The Elizabeth Cady Stanton Annual Birthday Tea, 10 November 1991, Gould Hotel, Seneca Falls, New York. Sponsored by the Elizabeth Cady Stanton Foundation.

Mother Earth, Creator of Life

1. Matilda Joslyn Gage, "The Onondaga Indians." *The* (New York) *Evening Post,* 3 November 1875. Scrapbook of Gage's Published Newspaper Articles, Matilda Joslyn Gage Collection, Schlesinger Library, Radcliffe College, Cambridge, Mass.

2. Harriet Maxwell Converse, *Myths and Legends of the New York State Iroquois.* Albany: New York State Museum, 1908, pp. 63-64.

3. Arthur C. Parker, "Iroquois Uses of Maize and Other Food Plants," *Education Department Bulletin,* No. 482, 1 November 1910, Albany: University of the State of New York, 1910, p. 27.

4. James. E. Seaver, *A Narrative of the life of Mrs. Mary Jemison, Who was taken by the Indians, in the year 1755, when only about twelve years of age, and has continued to reside amongst them to the present time.* J.D. Bemis & Co., 1824, pp. 35-36, 69-71.

5. Gage, "The Onondaga Indians."

6. Ibid.

7. W. M. Beauchamp, "The New Religion of the Iroquois," *The Journal of American Folk-Lore.* Vol. 10, No. 38, July-September 1897, p. 177.

8. "The Creation Story" in *Legends of Our Nations.* Cornwall Island, Ontario: North American Indian Travelling College, n.d., p. 76.

9. Stanton, "The Matriarchate or Mother-Age."

10. Ibid.

11. Elizabeth Cady Stanton's "Blessing" in Margaret Stanton Lawrence "Reminiscences," Stanton Collection, Vassar College Library, Poughkeepsie, New York.

12. The notable exception was Mary Baker Eddy, the one United States woman to establish a continuing religion (The First Church of Christ, Scientist). Mrs. Eddy__before Santon and Gage__recognized the Motherhood and Fatherhood.

13. "Condensation of the Opening Address sent by the Mohawk Nation and the Haudenosaunee Grand Council to the Fourth Russell Tribunal, Rotterdam, The Netherlands, November 1980," *Northeast Indian Quarterly*, Fall 1987, p. 8. From the Thanksgiving Address.

14. Stanton, "The Matriarchate or Mother-Age."

15. Matilda Joslyn Gage, "Msickquatash," *Appleton's Journal*, [1875]. Scrapbook of Gage's Published Newspaper Articles, Matilda Joslyn Gage Collection, Schlesinger Library, Radcliffe College, Cambridge, Mass.

16. Matilda Joslyn Gage, [Alcor], "Green Corn Dance of The Onondagas." To the Editor of the [New York] *Evening Mail*, n.d. Scrapbook of Gage's Published Newspaper Articles, Matilda Joslyn Gage Collection, Schlesinger Library, Radcliffe College, Cambridge, Mass.

17. Gage, "The Onondaga Indians."

18. Hattie A. Burr, *The Woman Suffrage Cook Book*, N.p.: 1886; reprinted in Robert B. Thomas, *The Old Farmer's Almanac*, 1968.

19. Matilda Joslyn Gage, editorial, "Indian Citizenship," (Syracuse, New York) *National Citizen and Ballot Box*, May 1878.

20. Stanton, "Elizabeth Cady Stanton on Socialism."

From Subordination to Cooperation

1. Stanton, *The Woman's Bible*, p. 7.

2. Stanton, "The Matriarchate or Mother-Age."

3. Stanton et al, *History of Woman Suffrage* Vol. 1, pp. 70-71.

4. Stanton, "The Matriarchate or Mother-Age."

5. Fletcher, "The Legal Conditions of Indian Women," pp. 238-239.

6. Ibid.

7. Burnham, Carrie S., *Tract No. 5: Common Law*, N.p.: n.d., Women's Rights Vol. 2, Department of Rare Books, Olin Library, Cornell University, Ithaca, N.Y. When Burnham applied to the University of Pennsylvania to study law, Spencer Miller, who was dean of the law department, said that if women or Negroes were admitted, he would resign. Ultimately she won and studied law there.

8. Burnham cites the following: Blackstone, Vol. 1, p. 463; Vol. 4, p. 212; Bouvier's *Institutes*, pp. 15-157; "Decisions of English courts in 1612," quoted in *7 Mod. Rep.*, p. 264.

9. The State vs. Jesse Black, Supreme Court of North Carolina, Raleigh. 60 N.C. 266; 1864. R. Emerson and Russell P. Dobash, "Wives: The 'Appropriate' Victims of Marital Violence," *Victimology: An International Journal* 2 (1977-78): pp. 430-431.

10. Myrtle, p. 138.

11. W.M. Beauchamp, "The New Religion of the Iroquois," p. 178.

12. Fletcher, "The Legal Conditions of Indian Women," p. 238.

13. For a more complete account, see Sally Roesch Wagner, "The Iroquois Confederacy: a Native American Model for Non-sexist Men," *Changing Men*, Vol. 19, Spring-Summer 1988, pp. 32-34.

14. Gage, *Woman, Church and State*, p. 101.

15. Mary Elizabeth Beauchamp, "Letter to the Editor," *Skaneateles Democrat*, 10 April 1883, Beauchamp File, Onondaga Historical Association, Syracuse, New York.

16. Elias Johnson, *Legends, Traditions and Laws of the Iroquois*. Lockport, New York: Union Printing and Publishing Co., 1881, pp. 22-23.

17. J. N. B. Hewitt, "Status of Women in Iroquois Polity before 1784" in *Annual Report of the Board of Regents of the Smithsonian Institution for 1932*. Washington, D.C.: U.S. Government Printing Office, 1933, pp. 482-483.

18. I'm choosing here to look at status as Ann Eastlack Schafer did in her 1941 MA thesis in Anthropology for the University of Pennsylvania, "The Status of Iroquois Women." Schafer defines status as simply, the "collection of rights and duties" of "all the positions which she occupies," as distinct from the Iroquois woman's role: "the dynamic aspect of a status."

19. Matilda Joslyn Gage, "The Mother of His Children," (San Francisco) *Pioneer*, 9 November 1871. Scrapbook of Gage's Published Newspaper Articles, Matilda Joslyn Gage Collection, Schlesinger Library, Radcliffe College, Cambridge, Mass.

20. Gage, *Woman, Church and State*, p. 5.

21. Joshua V. H. Clark, *Onondaga or Reminiscences*. Syracuse, New York: Stoddard and Babcock, 1849, Vol. 1, pp. 49-50.

22. William Alexander, *History of Women*. Philadelphia: Published by J.H. Dobelbower, 1796.

23. Carroll E. Smith, *Syracuse, Village and City*. Local History Leaflet No. 16. Syracuse, New York: Onondaga Historical Association, October 1897, p. 69.

24. Rose N. Yawger, *The Indian and the Pioneer: An Historical Study*. Syracuse, New York: C. W. Bardeen, 1893, p. 39.

25. Myrtle, *The Iroquois*, pp. 85-6.

26. Horatio Hale, ed., *The Iroquois Book of Rights*, Philadelphia: D.G. Brinton, 1883; reprint ed. Toronto: University of Toronto Press, l963, pp. 141, 143.

27. Ibid., p. 168.

29. Ibid.

31. Gage, "The Remnant of the Five Nations: Woman's Rights Among the Indians."

32. Gage, *Woman, Church and State*, p. 5.

33. Fletcher, pp. 239-240.

34. Ibid., p. 238.

35. Emma Vignal Borglum, *The Experience at Crow Creek: A Sioux Indian Reservation at South Dakota*. Collection of the Manuscript Division, Library of Congress.

36. Myrtle, pp. 85-6.

37. Burnham, Carrie S.

38. Lewis Henry Morgan, *League of the Ho-De-No-Sau-Nee or Iroquois*. Herbert M. Lloyd [ed.] New York: Dodd, Mead and Co., 1904, p. 80.

39. Ibid., p. 317.

40. Schoolcraft, Henry R., *Notes on the Iroquois*. New York: Bartlett & Welford, 1846, pp. 88-89.

41. "Report of the Proceedings of the Mississippi Bar Association, January 6, 1891," printed in *The Albany Law Journal*, 5 March 1892.

42. Stanton et al., *History of Woman Suffrage* Vol. 1, pp. 70-71.

43. Gage, *Speech of Mrs. M.E.J. Gage at the Woman's Rights Convention held at Syracuse, September 1852*.

44. Fletcher, pp. 238-239.

45. Ibid.

Political Outsider and Lawbreaker

1. Stanton et al., *History of Woman Suffrage* Vol. 3, pp. 70-71.

2. Matilda Joslyn Gage, "Woman's Rights Catechism," *The* (Fayetteville, N.Y.) *Weekly Recorder*, 27 July 1871.

3. *New Northwest*, (Portland, Oregon), 8 March 1872, p. 3. The chapter on "Trials and Decisions" in Stanton, et al., *History of Woman Suffrage*, Vol. 2, New York: Fowler and Wells, 1882; reprint ed., Salem, New Hampshire: Ayer Company Publishers, Inc., 1985, pp. 586-755.

4. *An Account of the Proceedings of the Trial of Susan B. Anthony, on the Charge of Illegal Voting, at the Presidential Election in November, 1872.*

Rochester: Daily Democrat and Chronicle Book Print, 1874; reprint ed., New York: Arno Press, 1974; Stanton, Anthony and Gage, *History of Woman Suffrage*, Vol. 2, p. 689.

5. Stanton, et al., *History of Woman Suffrage*, Vol. 2, p. 689.

6. *Minor v. Happersett*, 53 Mo., 58, and 21 Wallace, 162, 1874; "Trials and Decisions" in Stanton et al., *History of Woman Suffrage*, Vol. 2, pp. 586-755.

7. Stanton et al., *History of Woman Suffrage*, Vol. 3, p. 20.

8. Stanton, "The Matriarchate or Mother-Age."

9. Gage, "The Remnant of the Five Nations: Woman's Rights Among the Indians."

10. Morgan, *League*, p. 82.

11. Hewitt, "Status of Women in Iroquois Polity before 1784," pp. 478-479.

12. Barbara A. Mann and Jerry L. Fields, "A Sign in the Sky: Dating the League of the Haudenosaunee," *American Indian Quarterly*, Vol. 21, No. 5, Summer 1997, pp. 423-449.

13. Tehanetorens, "Wampum Belts," Six Nations Museum, Onchiota, New York, n.d.; reprint ed. Ontario, Canada: Iroqrafts, Ltd., 1983.

14. Arthur C. Parker, *The Life of General Ely S. Parker*. Buffalo, New York: Buffalo Historical Society, 1919, quoted in "Her Word Was Law, Excerpts from Parker," *Indian Roots of American Democracy*, Vol. 4, No. 4, Winter 1887, p. 70.

15. Hewitt, "Status of Women in Iroquois Polity before 1784," p. 481.

16. Myrtle, p. 303.

17. Ibid., p. 162.

18. Ibid., p. 42.

19. Matilda Joslyn Gage to "My dear Helen," 11 December 1893.

20. Quoted in George S. Snyderman, "Behind the Tree of Peace: A Sociological Analysis of Iroquois Warfare," doctoral dissertation, University of Pennsylvania, 1948, p. 21.

21. Snyderman, p. 21.

22. Gage, "The Remnant of the Five Nations: Woman's Rights Among the Indians."

23. Gage, *Woman, Church and State*, p. 10.

24. Myrtle, p. 161.

25. Gage, *Woman, Church and State*, p. 5.

26. Fletcher, p. 239.

27. William L. Stone, *The Life and Times of Red Jacket or Sa-Go-Ye-Wat-Ha; Being the Sequel to the History of the Six Nations*. New York and London: Wiley and Putnam, 1841, pp. 61-62.

28. Ibid., pp. 155-156.

29. Ibid., pp. 119-120.

30. *Syracuse Journal*, 10 January 1866.

31. Arthur C. Parker, "Woman's Rights in America Five Hundred Years Ago," *Albany Press*, 11 April 1909.

32. Gage, "Indian Citizenship."

33. Resolution adopted by the National Woman Suffrage Association Convention, January, 1878 in *The National Citizen and Ballot Box*, August 1878.

34. Gage, *Woman, Church and State*, p. 6.

35. Parker, "Woman's Rights in America Five Hundred Years Ago."

36. Gage, *Woman, Church and State*, p. 6.

37. Stanton, "The Matriarchate or Mother-Age."

Afterword

1. Julius Cook, biographical sketch of Ray Fadden in *New Voices from the Longhouse: an Anthology of Contemporary Iroquois Writing*, edited by Joseph Bruchac. Greenfield Center, New York: The Greenfield Review Press, 1989, p. 96.

Bibliography

Adams, Charles Francis, *Familiar Letters of John Adams and His Wife, Abigail Adams, During the Revolution*, 1876.

Alexander, William, *History of Women*. Philadelphia: Published by J.H. Dobelbower, 1796.

Allen, Paula Gunn, *The Sacred Hoop: Recovering the Feminine in American Indian Traditions*. Boston: Beacon Press, 1986.

The (Washington, D.C.) *Alpha*, May 1880, p. 6.

An Account of the Proceedings of the Trial of Susan B. Anthony, on the Charge of Illegal Voting, at the Presidential Election in November, 1872. Rochester: Daily Democrat and Chronicle Book Print, 1874; reprint ed., New York: Arno Press, 1974.

Banner, Lois, *Elizabeth Cady Stanton: A Radical for Woman's Rights*. Boston: Little Brown and Company, 1980.

Barreiro, Jose, "Challenging the Eurocentric Notion" in *Indian Roots of American Democracy*. Ithaca, N.Y.: Northeast Indian Quarterly, 1988, pp. xii-xvi.

Beauchamp, Mary Elizabeth, Letter to the Editor, *Skaneateles Democrat*, 10 April 1883, Beauchamp File, Onondaga Historical Association, Syracuse, New York.

Beauchamp, William M., *Iroquois Folk Lore Gathered from the Six Nations of New York*. Empire State Historical Publication 31, n.d.; reprint ed. Port Washington, N.Y.: Ira J. Friedman Division, Kennikat Press, n.d.

_____, "Iroquois Women," *The Journal of American Folk-Lore*. April-June 1900, Vol. 13, No. 49, pp. 81-91.

_____, "The New Religion of the Iroquois," *The Journal of American Folk-Lore*. Vol. 10, No. 38, July-September 1897, pp. 169-180.

Blatch, Harriet Stanton, "Voluntary Motherhood." *The National Bulletin* Vol. 1, No. 5, February 1891.

Borglum, Emma Vignal, *The Experience at Crow Creek: A Sioux Indian Reservation at South Dakota*. Collection of the Manuscript Division, Library of Congress.

Burnham, Carrie S., *Tract No. 5: Common Law* (N.p, n.d.), Women's Rights Vol. 2, Department of Rare Books, Olin Library, Cornell University, Ithaca, N.Y.

Burr, Hattie A. *The Woman Suffrage Cook Book*. N.p.: 1886; reprinted in Thomas, Robert B. The Old Farmer's Almanac, 1968.

"Capt. Oren Tyler," 1906. Seneca Falls Historical Society Papers, Seneca Falls, New York.

Caswell, Harriet S., *Our life Among The Iroquois Indians*. Boston and Chicago: Congregational Sunday-School and Publishing Society, 1892.

Clark, Joshua V. H., *Onondaga or Reminiscences*. Syracuse, New York: Stoddard and Babcock, 1849.

Col. Proctor's (1791) Journal. Harrisburg, Pa.: Pennsylvania Archives 2nd Series, 4, pp. 502-509.

"Condensation of the Opening Address sent by the Mohawk Nation and the Haudenosaunee Grand Council to the Fourth Russell Tribunal, Rotterdam, The Netherlands, November 1980." *Northeast Indian Quarterly*, Fall 1987, p. 8.

Converse, Harriet Maxwell, "New York's Indians," *New York Herald*, 2 February n.d. Writings of H. M. Converse and Miscellaneous Scrapbook of Ely S. Parker, p. 109. New York State Archives, Albany, New York.

_____, *Myths and Legends of the New York State Iroquois*. Albany: New York State Museum, 1908.

Cook, Julius, biographical sketch of Ray Fadden in Joseph Bruchac [ed.] *New Voices from the Longhouse: an Anthology of Contemporary Iroquois Writing*. Greenfield Center, New York: The Greenfield Review Press, 1989.

"The Creation Story" in *Legends of Our Nations*. Cornwall Island, Ontario: North American Indian Travelling College, n.d.

Dobash, R. Emerson and Russell P., "Wives: The 'Appropriate' Victims of Marital Violence," *Victimology: An International Journal* 2, 1977-78, pp. 430-431.

Eaton, Harriet Phillips, letters to Matilda Joslyn Gage [1890s]. Matilda Joslyn Gage Collection, Schlesinger Library, Radcliffe College, Cambridge, Mass.

Evening Post (New York), Commentary on "The Remnant of the Five Nations: Woman's Rights Among the Indians" by Matilda Joslyn Gage, 24 September, 1875. Matilda Joslyn Gage Collection, Schlesinger Library, Radcliffe College, Cambridge, Mass.

Fadden, Ray, "Fourteen Strings of Purple Wampum to Writers about Indians," in Joseph Bruchac [ed.] *New Voices from the Longhouse: an Anthology of Contemporary Iroquois Writing*. Greenfield Center, New York: The Greenfield Review Press, 1989, pp. 97-98.

Fletcher, Alice, "The Legal Conditions of Indian Women," *Report of the International Council of Women, Assembled by the National Woman Suffrage Association . . . 1888*. Washington, D.C.: Rufus H. Darby, 1888, pp. 237-241.

Flexner, Eleanor, *Century of Struggle*. New York: Atheneum, 1974.

Gage, Matilda Joslyn, [Alcor], "Green Corn Dance of The Onondagas," To the Editor of the [New York] *Evening Mail* n.d. Scrapbook of Gage's Published Newspaper Articles, Matilda Joslyn Gage Collection, Schlesinger Library, Radcliffe College, Cambridge, Mass.

_____, editorial, "Indian Citizenship," (Syracuse, New York) *National Citizen and Ballot Box*, May 1878.

_____, letter to "My dear Helen," 11 December 1893. Matilda Joslyn Gage Collection, Schlesinger Library, Radcliffe College, Cambridge, Mass.

_____, "Letter to the Editor," *Lucifer the Lightbearer*, 21 February 1890.

_____, "The Mother of his Children," (San Francisco) *Pioneer*, 9 November 1871. Scrapbook of Gage's Published Newspaper Articles, Matilda Joslyn Gage Collection, Schlesinger Library, Radcliffe College, Cambridge, Mass.

_____, "Msickquatash," *Appleton's Journal*, [1875]. Ibid.

_____, "The Onondaga Indians," *The* (New York) *Evening Post*, 3 November 1875. Ibid.

_____, "The Remnant of the Five Nations: Woman's Rights Among the Indians," *The* (New York) *Evening Post*, 24 September, 1875. Ibid.

_____, *Speech of Mrs. M.E.J. Gage at the Woman's Rights Convention held at Syracuse, September 1852*. Woman's Rights Tract No. 7. Syracuse: Master's Print, 1852.

_____, *Woman, Church and State*, Chicago: Charles Kerr, 1893; reprint ed., Aberdeen, South Dakota: Sky Carrier Press, 1998.

_____, "Woman in the Early Christian Church," *Report of the International Council of Women, Assembled by the National Woman Suffrage Association...1888*. Washington, D.C.: Rufus H. Darby, 1888, pp. 400-407.

_____, Woman's Rights Catechism, *The* (Fayetteville, N.Y.) *Weekly Recorder*, 27 July 1871.

Hale, Horatio, [ed.], *The Iroquois Book of Rights*. Philadelphia: D.G. Brinton, 1883; reprint ed. Toronto: University of Toronto Press, l963.

Hewitt, J. N. B., "Status of Women in Iroquois Polity before 1784" in *Annual Report of the Board of Regents of the Smithsonian Institution for 1932*. Washington, D.C.: U.S. Government Printing Office, 1933, pp. 475-488.

Johnson, Elias, *Legends, Traditions and Laws of the Iroquois*. Lockport, New York: Union Printing and Publishing Co., 1881.

Lucifer the Light Bearer, 13 March 1885.

Marcellus Observer, 8 July 1949.

Minor vs. Happersett, 53 Mo., 58, and 21 Wallace, 162, 1874.

Morgan, Lewis Henry, *League of the Ho-De-No-Sau-Nee or Iroquois*. Herbert M. Lloyd [ed.]. New York: Dodd, Mead and Co., 1904.

"My Daughter," *The* (New York) *Revolution*, 22 January 1868.

Myrtle, Minnie, *The Iroquois; or, The Bright Side of Indian Character*. New York: D. Appleton and Company, l855.

New Northwest, (Portland, Oregon), 8 March 1872.

New York Herald, 5 November 1905. Iroquois collection, Onondaga Historical Association, Syracuse, N.Y.

Onondaga Standard, 11 October 1890. Clipping File, Onondaga Historical Association, Syracuse, New York. Iroquois collection, Onondaga Historical Association, Syracuse, N.Y.

Onondaga Standard, 8 January 1946. Ibid.

Owen, Robert Dale, *Free Enquirer* Vol. 2, No. 1, p. 406; Vol. 2, No. 3, pp. 200-201; Vol. 2, No. 4, pp. 293-294; Vol. 2, No. 5, pp. 155, 264; Vol. 3, No. 1, p. 112.

_____, "The Moral Physiology" in *Birth Control and Morality in Nineteenth Century America: Two Discussions*. New York: Arno Press, 1972.

Paine, Tom, "Occasional Letter on the Female Sex," *Pennsylvania Magazine*, March 1775.

Parker, Arthur C., *The Life of General Ely S. Parker*. Buffalo, New York: Buffalo Historical Society, 1919, quoted in "Her Word Was Law, Excerpts from Parker," *Indian Roots of American Democracy*, Vol. IV, No. 4, Winter 1887, p. 70.

_____, "Iroquois Uses of Maize and Other Food Plants," *Education Department Bulletin*, No. 482, November 1, 1910. Albany: University of the State of New York, 1910.

_____, "Woman's Rights in America Five Hundred Years Ago," *Albany Press*, 11 April 1909.

Report of the International Council of Women . . . 1888. Washington, D.C.: Rufus H. Darby, Printer, 1888, pp. 237-241.

"Report of the Proceedings of the Mississippi Bar Association, January 6, 1891," printed in *The Albany Law Journal*, 5 March 1892.

Resolution adopted by the National Woman Suffrage Association Convention, January, 1878, in *The National Citizen and Ballot Box*, August 1878.

The Revolution (New York), 14 January 1869.

Schoolcraft, Henry R., *Notes on the Iroquois*. New York: Bartlett & Welford, 1846.

Seaver, James. E., *A Narrative of the life of Mrs. Mary Jemison, Who was taken by the Indians, in the year 1755, when only about twelve years of age, and has continued to reside amongst them to the present time*. J.D. Bemis & Co., 1824.

Shenandoah, Audrey. Speech at The Elizabeth Cady Stanton Annual Birthday Tea, 10 November 1991, Gould Hotel, Seneca Falls, New York. Sponsored by the Elizabeth Cady Stanton Foundation.

Should Women Vote? Important Affirmative Authority, N.p.: Equal Rights Association, n.d.

Skaneateles (New York) *Democrat*, 10 April 1883.

Smith, Carroll E., *Syracuse, Village and City*, Local History Leaflet No. 16. Syracuse, New York: Onondaga Historical Association, October 1897.

Smith, Erminnie A., *Myths of the Iroquois*, U. S. Bureau of American Ethnology, 2nd Annual Report, 1880-1881. Washington, D.C.: 1883; reprint ed. Ohsweken, Ontario, Canada: Iroqrafts, 1994.

Snyderman, George S., "Behind the Tree of Peace: A Sociological Analysis of Iroquois Warfare," Ph.D. Dissertation, University of Pennsylvania, 1948.

Spencer, Herbert, *Descriptive Sociology of England*. London: Williams and Morgate, [1873].

Stanton, Elizabeth Cady, "Blessing" in Margaret Stanton Lawrence "Reminiscences." Stanton Collection, Vassar College Library, Poughkeepsie, New York.

_____, Letter to Lucretia Mott, 19 July 1876, quoted in *History of Woman Suffrage* Vol. 3, pp. 45-47.

_____, Letters to Sara Underwood, 19 October 1889 and 9 May 1889. Stanton Papers, Special Collections, Vassar College Libraries, Poughkeepsie, New York.

_____, "If You Would be Vigorous and Healthy" in M. L. Holbrook, M.D., "Parturition Without Pain," appendix to George H. Napheys, *The Physical Life of Woman: Advice to the Maiden, Wife and Mother*. New York: M.A. Donohue and Company, 1927, pp. 365-366.

_____, "Elizabeth Cady Stanton on Socialism." Chicago: The Progressive Woman, 1898.

_____, Susan B. Anthony and Matilda Joslyn Gage, *History of Woman Suffrage* Vol. 1, New York: Fowler and Wells, 1881; Vol. 2, New York: Fowler and Wells, 1882; Vol. 3, Rochester: Susan B. Anthony, 1886; reprint ed., Salem, New Hampshire: Ayer Company Publishers, Inc., 1985.

_____, "The Matriarchate or Mother-Age," National Council of Women of the United States, Rachel Foster Avery [ed.], *Transactions of the National Council Women of the United States, Assembled in Washington, February 22 to 25, 1891*. Philadelphia, Pa.: 1891, pp. 218-227. Stanton-Anthony Papers 28:1013-1017. Also published in *The National Bulletin* 1, February 1891.

_____, *The Woman's Bible*. New York: European Publishing Company: 1895; reprint ed., Seattle: Coalition Task Force on Women and Religion, 1974.

Stanton, Henry B, *Random Recollections*. New York: MacGowan and Slipper, 1886.

The State vs. Jesse Black, Supreme Court of North Carolina, Raleigh. 60 N.C. 266; 1864.

Stern, Bernhard J., "The letter of Asher Wright to Lewis Henry Morgan," *American Anthropologist* 35, 1933.

Stone, William L., *The Life and Times of Red Jacket or Sa-Go-Ye-Wat-Ha; Being the Sequel to the History of the Six Nations*. New York and London: Wiley and Putnam, 1841.

Syracuse Journal, 10 January 1866.

Tehanetorens (Ray Fadden) to Sally Roesch Wagner, 23, November 1988. Personal Communication in collection of the author.

_____, "Wampum Belts," Six Nations Museum, Onchiota, New York, n.d.; reprint ed. Ontario, Canada: Iroqrafts, Ltd., 1983.

Turner, Orsamus, *Pioneer History of the account of the Holland Purchase of Western New York*. Buffalo: Geo. H. Derby and Co., 1850.

Vivian, John, "The Three Sisters: the nutritional balancing act of the Americas," *Mother Earth News*, February/March 2001, p. 50-53, 114.

Wagner, Sally Roesch, "The Iroquois Confederacy: a Native American Model for Non-sexist Men," *Changing Men* 19 (Spring/Summer 1988): 32-34.

_____, *A Time of Protest: Suffragists Challenge The Republic 1870-1887*. Aberdeen, S.Dak.: Sky Carrier Press, 1992.

Wallace, *Minor vs. Happersett*, 53 Mo., 58, and 21 Wallace, 162, 1874.

Yawger, Rose N., *The Indian and the Pioneer: An Historical Study*. Syracuse, New York: C.W. Bardeen, 1893.

Artist Credits

Page 5   Sally Roesch Wagner with grandson Tanner. Photo by Linda Roesch.

Page 9   Longhouse and the Tree of Peace. Artist Kahionhes (John Fadden), Turtle Clan, Mohawk nation. By permission of the artist.

Page 12   Mohawk holding wampum strings. Artist Kahionhes (John Fadden), Turtle Clan, Mohawk nation. By permission of the artist.

Page 21   Elizabeth Cady Stanton. *History of Woman Suffrage* Vol. 1, New York: Fowler and Wells, 1881; Vol. 2, New York: Fowler and Wells, 1882; Vol. 3, Rochester: Susan B. Anthony, 1886; reprint ed., Salem, New Hampshire: Ayer Company Publishers, Inc., 1985.

Page 25   Haudenosaunee family and longhouse. Artist Kahionhes (John Fadden), Turtle Clan, Mohawk nation. By permission of the artist.

Page 27   Woman makes offering. Artist Kahionhes (John Fadden), Turtle Clan, Mohawk nation. By permission of the artist.

Page 29   Iroquois woman and tree. Artist Kahionhes (John Fadden), Turtle Clan, Mohawk nation. By permission of the artist.

Page 31   War chief holding woman's nominating belt. Artist Kahionhes (John Fadden), Turtle Clan, Mohawk nation. By permission of the artist.

Page 33   Three generations of the Wolf Clan. Artist Kahionhes (John Fadden), Turtle Clan, Mohawk nation. By permission of the artist.

Page 40   Matilda Joslyn Gage. Collection of Sally Roesch Wagner.

Page 41   Corseted and ornamental non-persons in the eyes of the law. *Godey's Lady's Book*, June 1855.

Page 42   Lucretia Mott. *History of Woman Suffrage* Vol. 1, New York: Fowler and Wells, 1881; Vol. 2, New York: Fowler and Wells, 1882; Vol. 3, Rochester: Susan B. Anthony, 1886; reprint ed., Salem, New Hampshire: Ayer Company Publishers, Inc., 1985.

Page 43   Bloomers on an American woman. "The New Costume," *The Lily*, July 1851.

Page 43   Carolyn Mountpleasant, a Seneca woman, in traditional dress. "Gä-Hah-No, a Seneca Indian Girl in the costume of the Iroquois." From Lewis Henry Morgan, *League of the Ho-De-No-Sau-Nee or Iroquois*. 1901 edition.

Page 46   Woman of the Beaver Clan. Artist Kahionhes (John Fadden), Mohawk nation. By permission of the artist.

Page 47   Family lineage traditionally was reckoned through mother. Pictograph represents John Fadden—Turtle Clan, Eva—Wolf Clan, and two of their sons, Don and Dave—Wolf Clan. Artist Kahionhes (John Fadden), Mohawk nation. By permission of the artist.

Page 52 Mother Earth, Creator of Life. Artist Kahionhes (John Fadden), Mohawk nation. By permission of the artist.

Page 54 "And when'er some lucky maiden." Artist unknown. From Harriet S. Caswell, *Our Life Among the Iroquois Indians*, 1892.

Page 55 Ducks. Artist Kahionhes (John Fadden), Turtle Clan, Mohawk nation. By permission of the artist.

Page 60 Western women . . . [from] sacred creators of life-giving food to kitchen drudges. Drawing of the arrangement of the kitchen. From the first edition of *The American Woman's Home*, 1869.

Page 62 Iroquois woman cooking. Artist Kahionhes (John Fadden), Turtle Clan, Mohawk nation. By permission of the artist.

Page 70 Matilda Joslyn Gage. *History of Woman Suffrage* Vol. 1, New York: Fowler and Wells, 1881; Vol. 2, New York: Fowler and Wells, 1882; Vol. 3, Rochester: Susan B. Anthony, 1886; reprint ed., Salem, New Hampshire: Ayer Company Publishers, Inc., 1985.

Page 88 The emblem of power worn by the Sachem is a deer's antlers. Artist Kahionhes (John Fadden), Turtle Clan, Mohawk nation. By permission of the artist.

Page 91 We are left to answer for our women, who are to conclude what ought to be done by both Sachems and warriors. "Red Jacket, Sagoyawatha." Artist Kahionhes (John Fadden), Turtle Clan, Mohawk nation. By permission of the artist.

Page 96 Woman stands behind fire. Artist Kahionhes (John Fadden), Turtle Clan, Mohawk nation. By permission of the artist.

Page 116 Feather. Artist Kahionhes (John Fadden), Turtle Clan, Mohawk nation. By permission of the artist.

Index

Sally Roesch Wagner

One of the first women to receive a doctorate in this country for work in women's studies, (U.C. Santa Cruz), Sally Roesch Wagner was a founder of one of the first college women's studies programs (C.S.U. Sacramento). Having taught women's studies for twenty years, she now tours the country as a writer, lecturer and historical performer, "bringing to life" Matilda Joslyn Gage and her better-known woman's rights ally, Elizabeth Cady Stanton. A scholar in residence for the Women's Rights National Historical Park in Seneca Falls, New York during Celebrate 98, Wagner curated two exhibits, developed a curriculum and performed as both Elizabeth Cady Stanton and Matilda Joslyn Gage. Dr. Wagner is currently the Executive Director of the Matilda Joslyn Gage Foundation in Fayetteville, New York.

Wagner appeared as a "talking head" in the Ken Burns PBS documentary, "Not for Ourselves Alone: The Story of Elizabeth Cady Stanton and Susan B. Anthony" for which she wrote the accompanying faculty guide for PBS. She was also an historian in the PBS special, "One Woman, One Vote" and has been interviewed several times on National Public Radio's "All Things Considered" and "Democracy Now." The Jeanette K. Watson Women's Studies Distinguished Visiting Professor in the Humanities at Syracuse University in Spring 1997, Wagner has been a Research Affiliate of the Women's Resources and Research Center at the University of California, Davis and a consultant to the National Women's History Project.

The theme of her work has been telling the untold stories. The exhibit and her monograph of the same name, "She Who Holds the Sky: Matilda Joslyn Gage" reveals a suffragist written out of history because of her stand against the religious right 100 years ago, while her traveling exhibit and Women's Rights National Historical Park curriculum, "Sisters in Spirit," documents the influence of Haudenosaunee women on early women's rights activists. Wagner keynoted the opening session of the 1998 National Women's Studies Association convention with a lecture on this topic. She also briefed the First Lady, the White House Millennium Council and the press during Hillary Rodham Clinton's historic sites tour.

Her recent essays have appeared in *The Encyclopedia of Women and World Religion*; *Women Public Speakers in the United States, 1800-1925*; *Indian Roots of American Democracy*; *Iroquois Women: an Anthology*; and *Handbook of American Women's History*. Published articles include: *National Women's Studies Association Journal*, *On the Issues*, *Northeast Indian Quarterly*, *Indian Country Today*, *Hartford Courant*, *Women's History Network News*, *National NOW Times* and the *Sacramento Bee*.

Recent books include: *She Who Holds the Sky: Matilda Joslyn Gage;* a modern reader's edition of Matilda Joslyn Gage's 1893 classic, *Woman, Church and State*; *Daughters of Dakota* (six volume series); *The Untold Story of the Iroquois Influence on Early Feminists*; *A Time of Protest — Suffragists Challenge the Republic: 1870-1887* and *Celebrating Your Cultural Heritage by Telling the Untold Stories*.

These important books are available from your local bookstore.

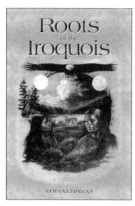

Roots of the
Iroquois
Tehanetorens
$9.95
978-1-57067-097-8

Legends of the
Iroquois
Tehanetorens
$9.95
978-1-57067-056-5

Wampum Belts of
the Iroquois
Tehanetorens
$9.95
978-1-57067-082-4

Basic Call To
Consciousness
edited by
Akwesasne Notes
$12.95
978-57067-159-3

Native Women of
Courage
in the Native Trailblazer
Series for young readers
Kelly Fournel
$9.95
978-0-97791-832-4

These books are also available from:
Book Publishing Company
PO Box 99 Summertown, TN 38483
1-888-260-8458
Free shipping and handling on all book orders.

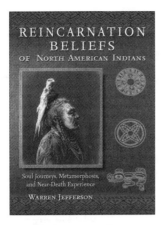

Reincarnation Beliefs of North American Indians
Warren Jefferson
$15.95
978-1-57067-212-5

Keeping Heart on Pine Ridge
Vic Glover
$9.95
978-1-57067-165-4

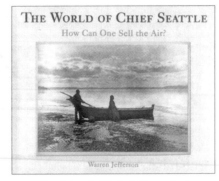

World of Chief Seattle
How Can One Sell the Air?
Warren Jefferson
$13.95
978-1-57067-095-4

These books are also available from:
Book Publishing Company
PO Box 99 Summertown, TN 38483
1-888-260-8458
Free shipping and handling on all book orders.